Unit 1 Australia

1 Welcome to Australia! ▸ pp. 6–7

Read Judith's blog on pp. 6–7 of your student's book and complete the sentences in your own words.

1 In the plane Judith felt very small and a bit scared because she saw how huge Australia was.

2 When Judith landed in Melbourne, she got a shock because in Cologne the weather had been hot and in Australia it was a cold day in winter.

3 School in Melbourne is different from school in Cologne for the following reasons: The school year has four terms. The school day begins at 8.30 and ends at 3.15. After school students do extracurriculars, then homework.

4 Something really scary happened to Judith in the bush. Before she went to bed one night, one of the girls saw a snake in Judith's sleeping bag and warned her about it just in time.

○* 2 What do you know? ▸ p. 8

Study the map on p. 8 of your student's book. Label as many states (2–7) and cities (B–G) as you can.

1 Western Australia
2 Northern Territory
3 South Australia
4 Queensland
5 New South Wales
6 Victoria
7 Tasmania

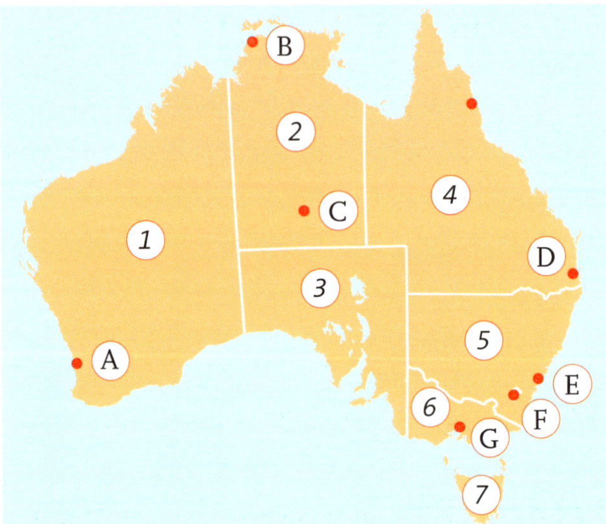

A Perth
B Darwin
C Alice Springs
D Brisbane
E Sydney
F Canberra
G Melbourne

3 LISTENING Captain James Cook ▸ p. 8 • WB (p. 71) 2

***a)** Listen the first time. Which answer is correct? Tick A, B or C.*

1 What is the text about?	A Cook's enemies.	B Cook's health.	☑ C Cook's biography.
2 James Cook was ...	A a Scottish sailor.	☑ B a British navigator[1].	C a British scientist.
3 When did Cook live?	☑ A In the 18th century.	B In the 19th century.	C In the 20th century.
4 Where did Cook die?	A In Australia.	B In Antarctica.	☑ C On Hawaii.

***b)** Listen again, then answer the questions in your exercise book. Make notes first.*

WB, pp. 50–53

1 When did Cook start his first sea journey and what did he succeed in doing?
2 Cook was a good captain and an excellent navigator. Name one fact each to support this.

[1] navigator ['nævɪgeɪtə] *Seefahrer*

*○ leichte Übung

4 Quiz: All about Down Under ▸ p. 9

a) Read pp. 8–9 of your student's book. Then tick answer A, B or C. You need the letters in brackets in b).

1 The capital of Australia is ...

A Melbourne. (P)	B ✓ Canberra. (G)	C Sydney. (D)

2 The first Europeans landed in Australia in the ... century.

A 14th (G)	B 15th (I)	C ✓ 16th (E)

3 In 1788 the British founded a colony in Port Jackson for ...

A farmers from Britain. (L)	B ✓ convicts from Britain. (R)	C Aborigines. (E)

4 The Commonwealth of Australia was founded in ...

A 1770. (S)	B 1788. (T)	C ✓ 1901. (B)

5 Which animals are found only in Australia?

A Kangaroo, emu, dolphin. (U)	B ✓ Koala, emu, kangaroo. (A)
C Koala, kangaroo, saltwater crocodile. (L)	

6 The Great Barrier Reef is along the coast of ...

A New South Wales. (O)	B Victoria. (H)	C ✓ Queensland. (S)

7 The Great Barrier Reef is ... long.

A ✓ more than 2,000 km (N)	B 1,500 km (H)	C 2000 miles (F)

8 A big problem for the people of Australia is ...

A crime in the cities. (M)	B ✓ the hole in the ozone layer. (I)	C dangerous animals. (E)

9 The name of the island south of Victoria is ...

A Adelaide. (M)	B Hobart. (P)	C ✓ Tasmania. (O)

10 Now most immigrants to Australia come from ...

A the USA. (O)	B ✓ Asia. (I)	C Britain. (E)

b) Write down the letters in brackets after your answers. If your answers are correct, you can put the letters in the right order to give you the name of a group of people: Aborigines.

5 REVISION Birds that don't fly (Simple present) ▸ p. 11 • GF (p. 145)

a) First find information about the emu. Then complete the sentences in the simple present.

	live	most things
doesn't	run	very fast
	fly	longer than ten years
don't	drink	only in Australia
	eat	a lot of water

1 The emu lives only in Australia.

2 It's a bird but it doesn't fly.

3 Emus run very fast, up to 50 km an hour.

4 They eat most things, even frogs and small snakes.

5 The emu drinks a lot of water. It enjoys playing in water too.

0305

6 Wild emus don't live longer than ten years but in animal parks they can live up to 20 years.

b) Find information about one of the following: the dolphin, the whale, the saltwater crocodile. Say what it does and doesn't do. In your exercise book, write a paragraph in the simple present.

6 REVISION A trip to Australia (Simple past) ▸ p. 11 • GF (p. 146)

a) *Complete the dialogue with the correct simple past form of the verbs in brackets.*

Will Hi, Jay! When did you get (you, get) back from Australia?

Jay Last Friday. We had (have) a really good time.

We even went (go) on a hike into the bush.

Will Well, that must have been fun! Did you see (you, see) any dangerous snakes or horrible insects?

Jay Well, we didn't see (not see) any,

but I was (be) pretty nervous all the time. I didn't sleep (not sleep) very well in the tent. We spent (spend) the last few days in Sydney.

Will Great! Did you do (you, do) the Bridge Climb?

Jay No, it looked (look) too scary. But we tried (try) surfing on Bondi

0406 Beach. I spent (spend) more time in the water than on the surfboard, I'm afraid!

b) *Imagine two friends have just returned from Australia. In your exercise book, write six questions that you would ask them about their holiday.*

Where did you stay? Did you …?

7 Extra STUDY SKILLS Charts ▸ p. 11 • SF (p. 126)

Write about the two charts in your exercise book. Look at p. 10 in your student's book for help. You can use phrases like:

This is a … chart. • It is about … • It shows … • It is divided into … slices. • A large majority / small minority is … • So, you can say …

1 **Reasons for visiting Australia (international visitors)**

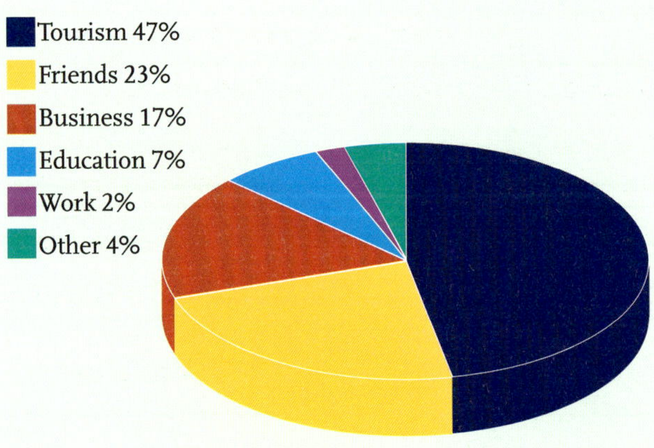

(Source: Tourism Research Australia 2009)

2 **Where visitors to Australia come from (in thousands)**

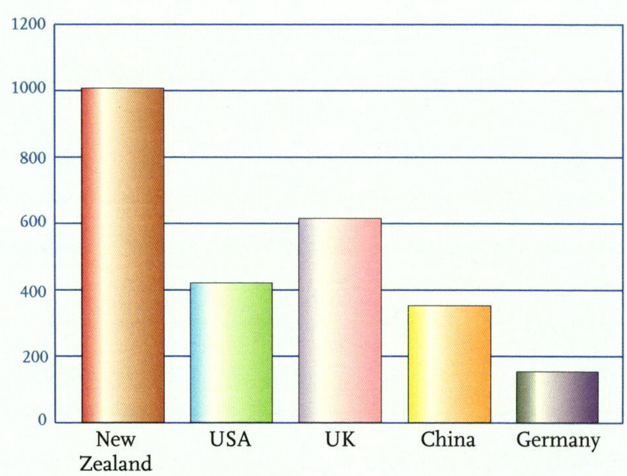

* schwierige Übung

8 SPEAKING COURSE

Part 1: Excuse me, … (Starting and continuing a conversation)

▸ p. 14 • WB (pp. 74–75) 🎧 3

a) *Mark the phrases you could use in the different steps of a conversation. More than one phrase is correct.*

Step 1: You want to start a conversation with somebody you don't know.

See you soon. • Hello! • Do you like …? • Excuse me, … • Hi! • Nice to meet you.

Step 2: You introduce yourself.

Bye! • I'm …, by the way. • Why don't you …? • My name's … • What about you?

Step 3: You start with a few general questions.

Can you say that again, please? • Have you ever … ? • Are you from here?

Step 4: You want to ask for information or help.

Can you tell me …? • Sorry, I didn't get that. • Do you know where …? • See you tomorrow.

Step 5: You tell someone that you don't understand, or you ask someone to repeat something.

Good to meet you. • Can you say that again, please? • Sorry, I didn't get that.

Step 6: You end the conversation.

Bye! • Sorry, I didn't get that. • See you later, maybe. • Thanks for your help.

b) *Ben, a student from the UK, wants to go to Bondi Beach, so he asks a girl on the street where he can buy some things that he needs. Complete the conversation with phrases from a). More than one answer is possible.*

Ben *Hi!/Excuse me, …*

Girl Hi! Going to the beach?

Ben Yes, but it's a bit too hot for me.

My name's Ben. / I'm Ben, by the way.

Girl Hi, Ben! I'm Lucy. Nice *to meet you*.
You're from the UK, right?

Ben Yes, I am. From London.

Are you from here/Sydney?

Girl Sure. I've lived here all my life. It's a great city.

Ben This is my first day here. I didn't think it would be so hot.

Can you tell me where / Do you know where I can get some sunscreen and a hat?

Girl Sure. There's a place that sells tourist stuff just round the corner, that way. Then you can slip, slop, slap.

Ben Sorry? *I didn't get that*. Slip what? Can you *say that again*, please?

Girl (*laughing*) Well, that's just what we do here – because of the sun. 'Slip! Slop! Slap!' You'll learn.

Ben Mmm? Oh. Well, *thanks for your help*. *Bye!*

'B, pp.
–64

c) *Now listen to the CD (🎧 3) and check your answers. The CD gives only one possible answer. Then listen again and read out the dialogue with your CD.*

0508
0509

d) **Extra** *Write a new dialogue between Ben, who now wants to rent[1] a bike for the day, and a girl he meets on the beach. Use phrases from the 6 steps in a) and ideas from b).*

[1] rent [rent] *mieten*

9 WORDS The right word ▸ p. 15

Choose the correct word and use it in the correct form to complete the sentences.

1 go • drive • ride : Jeannie lives in the outback. She can't _go_ anywhere by train or bus. She _rides_ her horse every day, but will she ever learn to _drive_ a car in a busy city?

2 make • do • take : Rob _does_ lots of sport, but now he's _taking_ a break from surfing because he has to work hard for school. At the moment he's _making_ breakfast before he goes to the beach with his books.

3 than • as • when : Jeannie learned to ride a bike _as_ a small child, _when_ she was only three. I think riding a dirt bike is more fun _than_ playing cricket.

4 make • do : There aren't many things you can _do_ in the outback and it is also hard to _make_ money there.

0609

Now you

What's good and bad about living 'in the middle of nowhere'? Make notes and prepare a two-minute talk for your class.

It's difficult to imagine living ... It must be very lonely, even scary ...

10 EVERYDAY ENGLISH WRITING An e-mail ▸ p. 15 • SF (p. 137)

You would like to know more about the School of the Air. Write to Jeannie and ask her how it works. Make notes first, then write your e-mail in your exercise book. Remember to use a good closing sentence.

Ideas: school – start and finish? • lessons – how many / long? • school subjects – which / how many? • homework / tests / exams? • school grades – when / how?

WB, pp. 59–62

Dear Jeannie,
I found your e-mail really interesting. I'd like to know more about ...

11 About Alice Springs (Indirect speech) ▸ p. 18 • WB (p. 76)

You met two teenagers who had been to Alice Springs. What did they tell you about it?

1 It's a small town in the desert.
2 I think about 25,000 people live there.
3 Visitors are always surprised at what they find there.

4 You can stay in a caravan, at a B & B or at a top hotel.
5 They have a great desert park with animals too.

1 The boy told me that _Alice Springs was a small town in the desert._

2 He thought that _about 25,000 people lived there._

3 He said that _visitors were always surprised at what they found there._

4 The girl said that _you could stay in a caravan, at a B&B or at a top hotel._

0611 5 She added that _they had a great desert park with animals too._

12 About Uluru (Indirect speech)

▸ p. 19 • WB (p. 76)

You asked two Australian teenagers you met about Uluru. What did they tell you?

1 Uluru is unbelievable. If you go there you'll never forget it.
2 I have a friend who has climbed it, but he won't do it again.
3 Uluru isn't like other rocks that tourists climb.

4 The Aborigines don't want people to climb Uluru.
5 It's against their culture and visitors have to respect that.
6 I hope we'll go to Uluru again, but we won't climb it.

1 The girl said that Uluru *was unbelievable, and that if I went there I would never forget it.*

2 She said that she *had a friend who had climbed it, but he wouldn't do it again.*

3 She added that Uluru *wasn't like other rocks that tourists climbed.*

4 The boy explained that *the Aborigines didn't want people to climb Uluru.*

5 He said that *it was against their culture and visitors had to respect that.*

0712 6 He hoped that *they would go to Uluru again, but they wouldn't climb it.*

13 MEDIATION
Climbing Sydney Harbour Bridge (Spoken English to German)

▸ p. 19 • WB (p. 76) 4

You are going to climb Sydney Harbour Bridge with your family. You call the Bridge hotline to find out answers to your parents' questions. Read the questions first. Then listen carefully and take notes in German. Answer your parents' questions.

1 Wie kommt man am besten zur Brücke? *Website überprüfen.*

2 Kann man mit dem Auto hinfahren? *Parken ist schwierig.*

3 Wann müssen wir dort sein? *15 Minuten vor dem Aufstieg.*

4 Gibt es eine Vorbereitung? *Ja.*

5 Wie lange dauert der Aufstieg insgesamt? *Ungefähr 2 Stunden.*

6 Gibt es Dinge, die wir nicht tun dürfen? *Nichts aus Metall mitbringen; keine Kameras oder Camcorder mitbringen.*

7 Was soll man anziehen? *Bequeme Sportschuhe, keine Sandalen, Lederschuhe, Schuhe, die offen sind.*

B, pp. –66

8 Was geschieht, wenn das Wetter schlecht ist? *Bei Gewitter oder sehr windigem Wetter: anderer Termin.*

14 ENGLISH FOR JOBS Basic telephone language ▸ p. 19 5

a) Cathy has seen a notice for a job in a souvenir shop in Alice Springs. She calls the shop to find out details.

First Cathy has to
- say who she wants to speak to (owner/manager),
- say her name,
- say why she's calling.

She wants to know
- where the shop is,
- what she would have to do,
- what hours she would have to work,
- how much they pay per hour,
- when she could start.

Complete the dialogue.

Manager Springs Souvenirs, Kelly speaking.

Cathy Hello. I'd like to speak to the owner or the manager, please.

Manager Speaking. I'm Kelly Potts, the manager.

Cathy Oh, hello. My name's Cathy Fox. I'm calling about the job in your shop.

Manager Good. We need a part-time assistant very soon.

Cathy Where is your shop, please?

Manager We're on Hartley Street, easy to find. There's a bus right to the door.

Cathy Oh, that's great. And what kind of work would I have to do?

Manager Oh, the usual things. We sell a lot of Aborigine art and hand-made articles. Books, maps, T-shirts, caps. All kinds of good quality souvenirs. You would have to answer customer questions, help with sizes and colours. That kind of thing. You don't need experience, but you have to be friendly and polite.

Cathy Great. I could do that. What hours would I have to work ? Weekends too?

Manager Well, we're open daily from 7 am to 10 pm. You can choose your hours. We close Sundays.

Cathy That sounds good. How much do you pay per hour?

Manager We pay $18 an hour. $22 per hour for evening work after 6 pm.

Cathy Fine. When could I start?

Manager Soon. If you're interested, come and see us today and we'll talk about details. 125 Hartley Street.

Cathy Thanks. I'll do that. Bye.

b) Listen to the CD (5) and check your answers.

c) Use words and phrases from a) to write a telephone dialogue in your exercise book. Josh Ashton, a student who is looking for a holiday job for six weeks, calls the fast food restaurant Burger Palace.

15 WORDS What do they mean? ▸ p. 19

*a) Explain these words. Use relative clauses with **who**, **which/that** or **where**.*

sleeping bag: A sleeping bag is something that you sleep in when you are camping.

sunscreen: Sunscreen is something that you put on your skin to protect it from the sun.

gallery: A gallery is a place where you can find lots of photos or pictures.

teenager: A teenager is a young person who is between 13 and 19 years old.

ancestor: An ancestor is a person in your family who lived many years ago.

0915 **orphan:** An orphan is a child who has no parents.

b) Use four words from a) in two or three sentences. Write them in your exercise book.

When you go on a hike in the Australian desert, you need ...

16 READING WORKING WITH THE TEXT In the outback ▸ pp. 20–24 • WB (pp. 71–72)

a) You can find the following words in the story in your student's book (pp. 20–23). How can you work out their meanings? Write A, B, C or D after the words. Then write the German meaning of the word. Check your answers with a dictionary if you are not sure.

A	B	C	D
from a picture	from the context	from words I already know	the word is like a German word

inland (*line* 23)	B, D	landeinwärts	prayer (*line* 160)	C	Gebet
sandy (*line* 27)	D	sandig	bones (*line* 172)	A	Knochen
cut (*line* 128)	C	Schnitt	steer (*line* 184)	D	Stier
pour (*line* 129)	B	fließen	flesh (*line* 257)	D	Fleisch
salty (*line* 136)	C	salzig	wound (*line* 260)	D	Wunde

b) Complete the sentences with true facts from the story. Use your own words.

1 Bill, Colm and Rusty are in the outback because it's Bill's job to repair the Dog Fence.

2 One day something is wrong with Rusty, but Bill knows what to do to save her.

3 Colm shoots the black boar because it had attacked Bill and his dog and hurt them badly.

4 After the attack, Colm knows that he has to get help for Bill as quickly as possible.

5 Colm has to run to the cattle station because the old car suddenly stops and he can't start it again.

WB, pp. …–58

*c) **Extra** In your exercise book, write an e-mail to a friend to tell him/her about the story. Say which parts you think are very exciting or boring.*

0917 I must tell you about a good story that I read in my English book. It's about a boy called Colm who ...
0918 It's especially exciting when ... I think the part where ... is a bit boring.

Skills Check 1

1 LISTENING Summer vacation 6

You are going to hear a conversation between Dan and his sister, Mel. First read the sentences, then listen and tick A, B or C. You will hear the recording only once.

1 The conversation takes place ...
- A on a train to Brisbane.
- [x] B on a plane to Melbourne.
- C on a bus to Darwin.

2 Their arrival time will be ...
- A 4.45.
- [x] B 14.45.
- C 14.54.

3 Why are Dan and Mel going there?
- A To go to summer camp.
- B To do a summer job.
- [x] C To visit family.

4 Mel and Ruth are ...
- A friends.
- B sisters.
- [x] C cousins.

5 During their vacation, Dan and Mel are planning to ...
- A go shopping.
- [x] B do lots of sport.
- C do lots of sightseeing.

6 They have already been to the City Museum ...
- A twice.
- [x] B three times.
- C four times.

2 LISTENING A day in the life of ... 7

You are going to hear part of a radio interview with two firefighters from the Queensland Fire Service. First read the sentences below, then listen to the recording. You will hear the recording twice.

a) *What do you hear about in the interview? Tick the correct box.*

- [ ] A koala rescue operation[1]
- [ ] The history of bushfires in Queensland
- [x] Why bushfires start

b) *Tick true or false.*

		True	*False*
1	Bob has been a firefighter for 30 years.		✓
2	Steve had a job with a furniture company before he became a firefighter.	✓	
3	On average, Queensland gets about 258 days of sunshine a year.		✓
4	In the dry[2] months firefighters work round the clock and get very little sleep.	✓	
5	Bob flies a helicopter with waterbombing equipment.		✓
6	Bushfires can start because of high temperatures and strong winds.	✓	
7	Eucalyptus forests burn easily because of the oil in the leaves.	✓	
8	The public can't do anything to stop bushfires.		✓
9	It's often difficult to make people leave their homes, although the fires are close.	✓	
10	Bob remembers saving a little girl's cat from the garden of her burnt house.		✓
11	Steve really likes being a firefighter.	✓	

[1] rescue operation ['reskjuː ˌɒpə'reɪʃn] *Rettungsaktion* [2] dry [draɪ] *trocken*

3 READING Sydney for everyone

a) Look at the text quickly. What is it about? Tick a box.

☐ Sydney's beaches ☐ Sydney's history ☑ Sydney's sights

b) Look at the text a second time. What information does it give? Tick the correct boxes.

☑ Opening times ☐ Prices ☑ Sights ☐ How to get there

SYDNEY FOR EVERYONE

Start at The Rocks

The Rocks is the oldest part of Sydney. Historically, it is an area of great importance as it is here that Sydney was founded, when the first British convicts were sent here in 1788. Because of its architecture from colonial times, it is often called Sydney's 'outdoor museum'. But today The Rocks has trendy boutiques, souvenir shops, cafés, restaurants and a weekend street market. The Sydney Visitor Centre is here too, so it's a good place to start your visit. **Open** from 9.30 am to 5.30 pm daily.

Climb Sydney Harbour Bridge

This is one of Sydney's most popular tourist attractions, called the 'Coat Hanger' by local people. It's easy to see why. Don't miss the challenge[1] of the Bridge Climb for an unforgettable experience!

The building of the bridge took about eight years. It was opened in 1932 and is used by about 150,000 vehicles daily. It takes about 80,000 litres of paint to paint the bridge once, and painting never stops. Did you know that the movie star Paul Hogan, better known as 'Crocodile Dundee', used to be a bridge painter before he became famous?

Opening times: 7 am to 8 pm daily.

Visit Sydney's historic buildings

Visit Elizabeth Farm in Parramatta, the oldest European building in Australia. Begun in 1793, the farm was the home of John and Elizabeth Macarthur, settlers[2] from England who became sheep farmers and started Australia's wool export industry. The old house, its furniture and its gardens show visitors how they used to live in the early 19th century. **Open** 9.30 am to 4 pm Friday to Sunday.

See a world-famous Sydney sight

The spectacular Sydney Opera House is situated in Sydney Harbour, surrounded by water on three sides. It was built by a Danish architect and was completed in 1973. Its design is a masterpiece of twentieth century architecture and a world-famous sight. By the way, not only opera but also concerts, theatre and ballet are performed here. If you take the 2-hour backstage tour, you can stand on the stage, where stars like Pavarotti or Michael Bublé have sung.

Visit Sydney Aquarium

Sydney Aquarium is one of the biggest in the world, with at least 6,000 fish, mostly Australian, and 650 different kinds of fish and marine animals. Visitors walk through underwater viewing tunnels to see marine life close up. Don't miss looking a huge shark[3] in the eye! **Opening times:** 9 am to 10 pm daily.

[1] challenge ['tʃæləndʒ] *Herausforderung* [2] settler ['setlə] *Siedler* [3] shark [ʃɑːk] *Hai*

READING

c) Now read the text for details. Is the information true (T), false (F) or not in the text (N)? Tick the correct box.

		T	F	N
1	The Rocks is an area of Sydney which reminds[1] visitors of Australia's colonial history.	✓		
2	Pilgrims from Britain arrived there in 1788.		✓	
3	There's a Rocks farmers' market on Fridays.			✓
4	Painting the Bridge is a never-ending job.	✓		
5	The Macarthurs were farmers from Scotland.		✓	
6	People call John Macarthur 'Father of the wool industry'.			✓
7	Sydney Harbour Bridge was started in 1924.	✓		
8	The Bridge is a railway bridge only.		✓	
9	Sydney Aquarium is home to 6,000 kinds of Australian fish.		✓	
10	Sydney Aquarium is the world's second biggest.			✓
11	Sydney Opera House is on a small island.		✓	
12	A Danish architect designed and built Sydney Opera House.	✓		
13	You can also see theatre productions at Sydney Opera House.	✓		
14	The backstage tour is one of the most interesting tours.			✓

WRITING

4 WRITING An e-mail or a summary

Complete a) or b):

a) *You are in Sydney. Write an interesting e-mail to an English friend about a day's sightseeing there (about 100 words). You may take some facts from 'Sydney for everyone' (p. 11), but use your own words. Remember your writing skills.*

[1] remind [rɪ'maɪnd] *erinnern*

***b)** Write a summary of the following story in about 150 words in your exercise book.*

A birthday surprise

It would be Nina's birthday soon. Her brother David and some friends had planned a birthday surprise for her – a trip to Kakadu National Park.

The group left early on their drive. They laughed, joked and talked about what they might do there, walking, rock climbing, fishing, swimming in a freshwater billabong[1], picknicking by the river.

'You must be joking! What about the crocodiles?' said David, who was always careful and never did anything dangerous.

Cathy said that most of the crocs in the park were freshwater crocs, smaller and not aggressive like 'salties'.

Mike argued that thousands of visitors went to Kakadu, but only two or three died each year in a croc attack. But Mike loved an adventure. He never said no to anything scary.

'I agree,' said Nina, who had always been the wild one in the family. 'Visitor safety is taken very seriously. Rangers check for crocs, even by helicopter. David, don't spoil our fun! You're always scared of something. Enjoy yourself more! I always say: No risk[2], no fun!'

'So they tell you not to swim for no reason, right? Why do you think there are crocodile warning signs everywhere? Not even the rangers can give you a guarantee that there will be no salties in the area. There are no guarantees,' David continued in a serious voice.

'Come on, guys, no more arguing. It's Nina's birthday tomorrow, and we're going to have a great time, eh, Nina?' said Mike laughing.

The rest of the day went well. In the evening they celebrated[3] Nina's birthday round a campfire. Nina was really happy.

The next day they made the short trip to the famous Jim Jim Falls. Nina wanted to see the beautiful natural pools under the waterfall. It was hot, and Mike was looking forward to a swim in the cool, clear water. The way there was a difficult climb over rocks. Mike and Nina loved rock climbing, so they soon left the others behind.

After some time David and Cathy couldn't see them any more. Nervously David shouted their names, but they were nowhere. 'This is crazy,' said David. 'We said we would all stay together.' Just then David fell and hurt his foot.

Cathy tried to calm him down, but she was worried too. 'They'll be back soon. We'll just wait here. You can't climb rocks anyway if your foot hurts.' But after two hours Mike and Nina still hadn't returned. David felt sick. He was so afraid. The minutes seemed like hours. The waiting went on ...

'Hey, you guys! Where were you? It was great up at the pool!' shouted Mike at last. They were back. David threw his arms round his sister. Nina didn't say much ...

Safely back home after the trip, when she was alone with David, Nina said, 'David, I have to tell you about what happened up at the falls. A huge saltie suddenly appeared on the edge[4] of the pool only ten metres away. I was terrified, Mike too – but he would never tell anybody. I couldn't move at first, but the croc came closer, so fast. We just dropped our stuff and ran away over the rocks – lucky that salties are bad climbers. We were too scared to go back, so we had to wait until it had gone – the worst two hours of my life. We could both have been eaten alive if we had jumped into the water. I'm so sorry about what I said – you know. You were right – there are no guarantees. And David, please don't tell Mum and Dad ...'

[1] billabong ['bɪləbɒŋ] *Seitenarm eines Flusses* [2] risk [rɪsk] *Risiko* [3] celebrate ['selɪbreɪt] *feiern* [4] edge [edʒ] *Rand, Ufer*

SPEAKING

5 SPEAKING Travelling 8

a) At a travel agency[1] in Australia your parents want you to ask about tours to Uluru. Listen (8) and speak to the assistant: ask questions or form sentences in the pauses.

Assistant G'day! How can I help you? …
You …

1 Grüße ebenfalls und frage, was man bei der Uluru-Tour alles sehen kann.
2 Frage, wann man aufstehen muss und wann die Tour losgeht.
3 Frage, wie lange die Tour dauert.
4 Frage, ob man auf der Tour Frühstück bekommt.
5 Frage, wie viel die Tour kostet und was im Preis inbegriffen ist.
6 Sage, du möchtest die Tour für zwei Erwachsene und zwei Jugendliche für morgen buchen.

b) Describe picture A or B: the background, the colours, the atmosphere. Say what the people in the picture are doing and how they maybe feel. Talk for about two minutes. You can record your speech.

I'd like to talk about picture A. The picture shows a scene in the outback …

MEDIATION

6 MEDIATION Berlin tours

An Australian student would like to go to Berlin for a weekend and he asks you what you can see there. You find a brochure about Berlin tours. Write down the most important things for him in English in your exercise book.

Entdecken Sie Berlin mit Alpha Tours – wann und wie Sie wollen

Genießen Sie eine geführte Tour mit dem Bus, Fahrrad oder zu Fuß zu den vielen Sehenswürdigkeiten der Hauptstadt. Wir organisieren Touren jeder Art für große und mittlere Reisegruppen sowie für kleine Gruppen von 8 bis 12 Personen – und das jeden Tag!
Wählen Sie Ihre spezielle Tour aus unseren vielen Angeboten aus!
Entdecken Sie u.a. folgende Highlights:
Regierungsviertel, Berliner Reichstag, Brandenburger Tor, Checkpoint Charlie, Mauerreste, Museumsinsel, Fernsehturm, Kaiser-Wilhelm-Gedächtniskirche, DDR Museum, Berliner Dom, Potsdamer Platz, Schloss Charlottenburg.

Wir bieten:
- moderne klimatisierte Reisebusse, neue bequeme Stadträder.
- Vormittags-, Nachmittags- und Abendtouren mit sämtlichen Eintrittsgeldern inklusive.
- genug Zeit für Fotostops und Erfrischungspausen bei allen Touren.
- bei Ganztagstouren ist auch ein Mittagessen enthalten.
- erfahrene, kundige Stadtführer/innen, die mehrere Fremdsprachen sprechen.

Besuchen Sie unsere Website, um Tourbeschreibungen, Preisinformationen, Adressen unserer Filialen und vieles mehr in Erfahrung zu bringen. Rufen Sie uns an oder kommen Sie ganz einfach vorbei!
Tel.: 030-529 487–0 / www.alphatoursberlin.com

[1] agency [ˈeɪdʒənsi] *Büro*

How did you do?

Check your answers to the exercises on p. 79. Then answer the questions below with Yes or No. If you tick No or would like some extra practice on that point, go to the exercise in your workbook (pp. 50–70).

1 LISTENING Summer vacation

	Yes	No	Exercise
1 Hast du dir vor dem Hören die Aufgabe gründlich durchgelesen?	☐	☐	1, 2
2 Hast du die Detailfragen ohne Probleme beantworten können?	☐	☐	3, 4

2 LISTENING A day in the life of ...

	Yes	No	Exercise
1 Konntest du nach dem 1. Hören beurteilen, um welches Thema es im Interview geht?	☐	☐	1, 2
2 Hast du dir beim 1. Hören Notizen gemacht (Zahlen, Daten, Namen)?	☐	☐	3, 5
3 Konntest du den australischen Akzent mühelos verstehen?	☐	☐	7
4 Konntest du dem Sprechtempo mühelos folgen?	☐	☐	8

3 READING Sydney for everyone

	Yes	No	Exercise
1 Konntest du schnell herausfinden, um was es in dem Text geht?	☐	☐	10, 16a
2 Hast du nach Schlüsselwörtern (*key words*) gesucht, um Antworten zu finden?	☐	☐	11, 12
3 Konntest du die Antworten auf Detailfragen problemlos finden?	☐	☐	13, 14
4 Hast du die Bedeutung unbekannter Wörter erschließen können?	☐	☐	15, 16b

4 a) WRITING E-mail

	Yes	No	Exercise
1 Hast du deine Ideen mithilfe eines *brainstorming* gesammelt und dazu Notizen gemacht?	☐	☐	17
2 Hast du einige der 5 *Ws* am Anfang deines Textes berücksichtigt?	☐	☐	18
3 Hast du Informationen aus Exercise 1 benutzt und mit eigenen Worten beschrieben?	☐	☐	19
4 Hast du passende Adjektive (z.B. *interesting, old*) für deine Beschreibungen benutzt?	☐	☐	33
5 Hast du hauptsächlich das *simple past* (z. B. *went, walked*) benutzt?	☐	☐	29
6 Hast du deine Wortstellung (z.B. in Nebensätzen) überprüft?	☐	☐	34
7 Hast du *linking words*, z.B. *but, after, before, while, because, although, so* benutzt?	☐	☐	31
8 Hast du deine Rechtschreibung/Grammatik überprüft und deine Fehler korrigiert?	☐	☐	35

4 b) WRITING A Summary

	Yes	No	Exercise
1 Hast du die wichtigsten Ereignisse erkannt und dazu Notizen gemacht?	☐	☐	17
2 Hast du die 5 *Ws* am Anfang deiner *summary* berücksichtigt?	☐	☐	18
3 Hast du die wichtigsten Ereignisse mit eigenen Worten wiedergegeben?	☐	☐	19, 30
4 Hast du den Unterschied zwischen dem *simple present* und *present progressive* beachtet?	☐	☐	28
5 Hast du deine Wortstellung (z.B. in Nebensätzen) überprüft?	☐	☐	34
6 Hast du *linking words*, z.B. *but, after, while, because, although, so* benutzt?	☐	☐	31
7 Hast du deine Rechtschreibung/Grammatik überprüft und deine Fehler korrigiert?	☐	☐	35

5 a) SPEAKING Travelling

	Yes	No	Exercise
1 Hast du problemlos passende Fragen mit *do/does* oder mit Fragewörtern bilden können?	☐	☐	22
2 Hast du in den Pausen schnell genug die passenden Fragen stellen können?	☐	☐	23b, 24c
3 Hast du die notwendigen Vokabeln gewusst?	☐	☐	23a

5 b) SPEAKING Travelling

	Yes	No	Exercise
1 Hast du bei der Bildbeschreibung Ortsangaben wie z. B. *on the right/left* usw. benutzt?	☐	☐	23a
2 Hast du Dinge, die die Personen gerade tun, mit dem *present progressive* beschrieben?	☐	☐	28
3 Hast du die Atmosphäre der Bilder mit passenden Adjektiven beschrieben?	☐	☐	33
4 Hast du wichtige Vokabeln für die Bildbeschreibung gewusst?	☐	☐	23a

6 MEDIATION Berlin tours

	Yes	No	Exercise
1 Hast du beachtet, mit eigenen Worten nur das Wesentliche weiterzugeben bzw. nicht alles wörtlich zu übersetzen?	☐	☐	25
2 Hast du (falls nötig) für unbekannte Wörter Umschreibungen benutzt (*paraphrasing*)?	☐	☐	32

Unit 2 The world of work

1 WORDS Jobs ▸ p. 32–33

a) *Collect the names of jobs on pp. 32–33 of your student's book. Write a list.*

theme park worker, chef, shop assistant, mechanic, police officer, make-up artist, childcare assistant, customer adviser, fitness instructor

b) *Complete what they say with job names from a).*

1 

I know quite a lot about cars. I'd like to be a mechanic.

4 

I enjoy cooking and I'd like to have my own restaurant one day. But first I'd like to be a chef in a big hotel kitchen.

2 

I'm quite artistic. I'd like to work in a theatre as a make-up artist.

5 

I like looking after children. I'd like to be a childcare assistant at a kindergarten.

3 

I like talking to customers and answering their questions. I'd like to be a customer adviser in a bank maybe.

6 

I'm a sporty person and I'm interested in health and fitness. Maybe I'd make a good fitness instructor.

1601
1602

c) *Make three lists in your exercise book. Write two more jobs for each list.*

Jobs inside	Jobs outside	Jobs inside and outside
office worker, teacher	gardener,	police officer,

2 WORDS Personal qualities ▸ p. 36

artistic • calm • careful • clever • confident • energetic • fit • friendly • good at … • hard-working • helpful • honest • likeable • logical • organized • polite • punctual • reliable • sporty

a) *Find five jobs and match them with these adjectives. Make sentences.*

1 I think a builder has to be strong, fit, reliable and hard-working.

2 I think a fitness instructor has to be likeable, fit, sporty, energetic and helpful.

3 I think a bank clerk has to be friendly, reliable, organized and good at Maths.

4 I think an office worker has to be organized, reliable and good at working in a team.

5 I think a nurse has to be careful, calm, reliable, punctual and friendly.

6 I think a police officer has to be calm, hard-working, reliable and honest.

b) *How do interviewers like their future apprentices to be? Write down what you think are the 'top ten' most important qualities in your exercise book.*

I think it's important to be …

3 WORDS What kind of person are you? ▸ p. 36

a) How do you think these people would describe you? Complete the sentences with words from the box. You can use adjectives and phrases from exercise 2 in your workbook (p. 16) or in your student's book (pp. 34–35).

a bit · quite · very · (not) always · sometimes · usually

1 Maybe my friends would describe me as ______

______

2 I think my family ______

______

3 Maybe my teachers ______

______

1703

b) Imagine that you are having an interview for a job that you would really like to do. The interviewer says: 'Tell me about yourself. Why do you want to work for us?' How would you answer this question? Think carefully, then prepare what you would say in a few sentences. Write in your exercise book.

I'm quite ... and I'm very interested in .../I think I'd be right for this job because ...

4 EVERYDAY ENGLISH MEDIATION Part-time jobs ▸ p. 37 · WB (p. 76)

You want to tell a friend about these part-time jobs in the UK. Write down notes. Say what you have to do in the jobs and what kind of people they are looking for.

1

High Street Café

We need a part-time waiter/waitress for our busy café. You will help in the kitchen, clean and lay tables, serve drinks, cakes, snacks, ice cream from 2 to 6 pm Saturday and Sunday. You should work quickly, be friendly, polite, tidy and good at Maths.
Pay above average.
Phone us on 01288 361255 for more information.

Job im Café: Kellner/in als Teilzeitkraft; Arbeiten in Küche, Servieren von Getränken und Snacks; 14.00–18.00 Uhr am Wochenende; freundliche, höfliche Person, die gut in Mathe ist

2

Are you a dog lover?

We walk dogs for owners who are ill or too busy to give their dogs long walks. We are looking for young people who like dogs and like walking. You will pick up the dog from its home and take it back to its owner on time.
Hours: 7 am to 1 pm or 1 pm to 7 pm in every kind of weather.
You should be reliable, friendly and good with dogs.
A bike to get you from walk to walk would be an advantage.
Apply to: dogwalkers@xlt.com

Hunde ausführen: 7.00–13.00 Uhr oder 13.00–19.00 Uhr bei jedem Wetter; junge Leute, die Hunde mögen und freundlich und zuverlässig sind; Rad wäre von Vorteil

WB, pp. 5–66

5 REVISION After school (Gerund as subject and object) ▸ p. 37

*Complete the sentences with your own ideas. Use gerunds, for example **I'll really enjoy working in a café.** or **Working in an office is something I've always wanted to do.***

1 When I leave school, I'll really enjoy ____________________

2 ____________________ is something I've always wanted to do.

3 ____________________ is very important for kids our age.

4 I can't really imagine ____________________

1805 5 I prefer __________ to __________ so that will be important when I apply for a job.

Now you

Think about these questions: What are you good at? What do you like doing? What are you used to doing? What are you not interested in? What do you hate doing? Write at least one sentence for each question in your exercise book.

6 REVISION Luke's dad wants him to ... (Infinitive constructions) ▸ p. 37

***a)** Luke doesn't really know what he wants to do next year. What do other people want him to do?*

1 *Dad*	'Do an interesting apprenticeship.'
2 *Mum*	'Work hard and get good exam results.'
3 *Brother*	'I think you should do volunteer work abroad for a year.'
4 *Girlfriend*	'Stay at home and get a job in a bank.'
5 *Best friend*	'Follow your dream and become a racing driver!'

1 Luke's dad wants *him to do an interesting apprenticeship.*

2 His mum expects *him to work hard and get good exam results.*

3 His brother told *him to do volunteer work abroad for a year.*

4 His girlfriend wants *him to stay at home and get a job in a bank.*

5 His best friend told *him to follow his dream and become a racing driver.*

***b)** Read Luke's questions on the right. Then complete the sentences with a question word + **to**-infinitive.*

1 What shall I do next year?
2 When shall I leave school?
3 What kind of job shall I apply for?
4 Whose advice shall I take?

1 Luke doesn't know *what to do next year.*

2 He can't decide *when to leave school.*

____

3 He doesn't know *what kind of job to apply for.*

____

4 He doesn't know *whose advice to take.*

1806 ____________________

7 EVERYDAY ENGLISH WRITING A job application form ▸ p. 37

a) Read about Jeff.

Jeff Miller is 15. He lives with his family and their cat at 7 Castle Road, Selby YO8 4TW. His home telephone number is 01757 809995. He hasn't got a mobile at the moment, but you can write to him at j.miller@axl.com. His hobbies are computers, reading, football and cycling. He knows a lot about bikes and often wins local cycle races.
He's been at Kingsway High School since 2005. He has GCSEs in English, Maths, German, Science and Geography. In July and August 2009 he worked at Samuel Sports. He served customers with sports shoes and equipment. Now he's looking for a holiday job for this summer. He's friendly, helpful and good with customers. He would like to work at Wilson Cycles, a big new bike centre in town.

b) Fill in Jeff's application form for Wilson Cycles with the correct information from a).

Job application form for WILSON CYCLES

PERSONAL DETAILS

First name(s) Jeff Last name Miller

Address 7 Castle Road, Selby YO8 4TW

Tel no (home) 01757 809995 Tel no (mobile) –

Email address j.miller@axl.com

WORK EXPERIENCE

Company	From	To	Job details
Samuel Sports	July 09	August 09	served customers with sports shoes
			and sports equipment

EDUCATION

School	From	To	School subjects
Kingsway High	2005	to date	GCSEs in English, Maths
School			German, Science, Geography

HOBBIES AND INTERESTS

Cycling and cycle races, computers, reading, football

c) Why does Jeff have a good chance of getting the job? Write a few sentences. You can use:
I think Jeff has a good chance because ... Another good thing is that he ...

8 STUDY SKILLS An English CV

p. 39 • SF (p. 136)

a) Which information should be on your English CV? Tick ten more boxes.

home address	✔	hobbies and interests	✔	telephone number	✔
first name and last name	✔	nationality		date of birth	
education to date	✔	e-mail address	✔	references	✔
qualifications	✔	work experience	✔	place of birth	
a personal statement	✔	sex		other skills	✔

b) Put the information that you have ticked in a) in the usual order for your English CV. If you are not sure, look at the CV on p. 38 of your student's book.

1 First name and last name
2 Home address
3 Telephone number
4 E-mail address
5 A personal statement
6 Education to date
7 Qualifications
8 Other skills
9 Work experience
10 Hobbies and interests
11 References

c) Use the CV on p. 38 of your student's book to write your own English CV, on the computer or in your exercise book.

INFO BOX

In Germany you include a photo with your CV, but not with your English CV for the UK.

9 STUDY SKILLS A letter of application

p. 39 • SF (p. 137)

a) Complete the information about formal letters.

1 If you start a formal letter with 'Dear Sir/Madam', you usually end it with 'Yours faithfully'.

2 If you know the name of the person, you start with 'Dear Mr/Ms ...' and end with 'Yours sincerely'.

b) In your exercise book, write Jeff's letter of application to Ms Roberts at Wilson Cycles with the sentences in a logical order. First, write 2–8 after the sentences. More than one answer is possible.

Dear Ms Roberts

In the last summer holidays I did work experience (six weeks) at Samuel Sports in George Street.	4
I enclose my CV.	2
I read your advertisement in the Selby Post and would like to apply for the job of assistant sales person.	1
I look forward to hearing from you soon.	7
I am very interested in cycles and have won local cycle races.	3
I enjoy serving customers and I do not mind working in the evenings or on Saturdays.	5
The manager at Samuel Sports will be happy to give me a reference.	6
Yours sincerely	8

10 SPEAKING COURSE Part 2: Anna's interview (Having a job interview)

▸ p. 41 • WB (p. 75) 🎧 9

a) Anna Wood is preparing for an interview for a summer job at a garden centre. Tick statements and questions which she could use at the interview.

- Can you tell me what I would have to do exactly? [x]
- Sorry I'm late. I missed the bus because my mum forgot to wake me. [ ]
- Would somebody help me? [x]
- Would I have to make the tea? [ ]
- Yes, I do. I look after my grandmother's garden. She has lots of trees and flowers. [x]
- Well, I think I would really like the work and I'd be good at it. [x]
- Is the pay good? [ ]
- My last job was awful. The manager wasn't fair. [ ]
- I worked in a busy office last summer. I learned a lot. But I like working outside more. [x]
- What are the hours of work? [x]
- I'm careful and reliable. I learn quickly, and I work hard when I'm interested in something. [x]

b) Imagine that you are Anna. Listen to the interviewer on your CD (🎧 9) and answer her questions. Read the sentences that you have ticked in a) again before you start. Do the exercise at least twice.

WB, pp. 63–64

Interviewer Good morning. I'm Jane Ashton, the manager. You're Anna Wood, is that right? Thank you for your application. Did you find us easily?
You Yes, thanks. It was no problem.
Interviewer Now, why did you apply for a gardening job?
You …

2110

11 REVISION After the interview (Indirect speech)

▸ p. 42 • WB (p. 76)

What did Anna tell the interviewer? Complete the sentences. Remember to change the tense.

1. I'm careful, reliable and hard-working.
2. I like working outside.
3. I have some work experience.
4. I do the garden work for my grandmother.
5. I enjoy looking after plants and trees.
6. I can work at weekends.
7. I don't mind working alone.

1. At the interview Anna said that she __was__ careful, reliable and hard-working.
2. She told Ms Ashton that she __liked__ working outside.
3. She also said that she __had__ some work experience.
4. She told her that she __did__ the garden work for her grandmother.
5. She said that she __enjoyed__ looking after plants and trees.
6. She told Ms Ashton that she __could__ work at weekends too.
7. She also said that she __didn't__ mind working alone.

2111

12 Interview tips (Indirect speech: commands and requests) ▸ p. 42 • WB (p. 77)

a) *Before Jeff Miller went for his interview, he met his friend Jamal, who gave him a few good tips. Read what Jamal said.*

'I've had a few interviews and I've always said something wrong or done something silly because I was too nervous. I'll give you a few tips:

[1] *Be punctual* and [2] *don't forget* to turn off your phone. My phone once rang in the middle of an interview. I felt awful. [3] Don't show that you're nervous, and [4] ask a few clever questions. [5] Look the interviewer in the eye and [6] don't talk too much. I usually do that! [7] Can you phone me after the interview to tell me the news? [8] And if you get the job, can you give me some money?'

b) *Now complete the text.*

[1] Jamal *told Jeff to be* punctual and [2] *not to forget* to turn off his phone.

[3] He also *told Jeff not to show* that he was nervous and [4] told *him to ask* a few clever questions. [5] Then he *told him to look* the interviewer in the eye and [6] *not to talk* too much. [7] Before Jeff had to go, Jamal *asked him to phone* him after the

2212 interview. [8] Jamal also *asked Jeff to give* him some money – if he got the job.

Now you

Think of four more tips that you would give a friend before an interview. Write them in your exercise book.

I would tell him/her to .../I'd tell him/her not to ...

13 Interview questions (Indirect speech: questions with question words) ▸ p. 43 • WB (p. 77)

Ms Roberts asked Jeff these questions at the interview.

1. Why do you want to work for us?
2. What do you know about Wilson Cycles?
3. What makes one bike more expensive than another?
4. What are your strengths?
5. How good are you with customers?
6. When can you start if we offer you the job?

Later at home, Jeff told his mum what the interviewer had asked. What did he say?

1 Ms Roberts asked me *why I wanted to work for them.*

2 She asked me *what I knew about Wilson Cycles.*

3 She wanted to know *what made one bike more expensive than another.*

4 She asked me *what my strengths were.*

5 Then she asked *me how good I was with customers.*

2213 6 She also wanted to know *when I could start if they offered me the job.*

14 What did Jeff ask? (Indirect speech: yes/no questions)

▸ p. 43 • WB (p. 77)

Jamal wanted to know what questions Jeff had asked at the interview. These were some of his questions.

1 'Will there be any training first?'
2 'Do you sell very expensive racing bikes?'
3 'Do I have to know all the technical details?'
4 'Is there a repair service?'
5 'Can I repair my own bike in the lunch breaks?'
6 'Will I be allowed to try out the new bikes?'

I asked *if there would be any training first.*

1 I asked *if there would be any training first.*

2 I asked *if they sold very expensive racing bikes.*

3 I asked *if I had to know all the technical details.*

4 I wanted to know *if there was a repair service.*

5 I asked *if I could repair my own bike in the lunch breaks.*

2314 6 I wanted to know *if I would be allowed to try out the new bikes.*

15 WORDS Getting a job

▸ p. 43

apply • apprenticeship • candidate • confident • CV • *decisions* • details • education • enclose • experience • fill in • future • pay • polite • qualifications • skills • training

a) *Complete the text with words from the box.*

Before you leave school there are some important *decisions* to make, but whatever job you do in the *future*, you'll need some *qualifications*. Maybe you'd like to do an *apprenticeship* for two or three years. The *pay* won't be good, but you'll get special job *training* and you'll learn some useful *skills*. When you *apply* for a job, you usually have to *fill in* an application form which asks for your personal *details*, your school *education* and your work *experience*. You should also *enclose* your *CV* and a formal letter of application. If you are an interesting *candidate*, the company might invite you to an interview. You should be well prepared, friendly and *polite*, and be *confident* about what you are good at. Good luck!

b) *Complete the sentences with a word from the same family as the word in brackets.*

1 Jeff read an *advertisement* (advertise) for a summer job at Wilson Cycles.

2 He sent an *application* (apply) to Ms Roberts, who invited him to an interview.

3 Jeff is a very *energetic* (energy) person and he has a lot of *strengths* (strong).

4 For the interview he dressed *suitably* (suitable) and showed that he was *organized* (organize).

2315 5 He hopes Ms Roberts was *impressed* (impress).

16 ENGLISH FOR JOBS LISTENING Phone calls ▸ p. 43 • WB (p. 71) 10

Test

Mrs Holby is a busy manager. Ben, her assistant, writes the times of her appointments and interviews in an appointments diary. Listen to the telephone calls, and write the necessary changes in the diary.

Monday	Tuesday	Wednesday	Thursday	Friday
~~10.30 Interview: Ms Jane Morton~~	~~10.15 Mr D. Thomas, (Bell Electronics)~~ 10.30 Mr Tim Brown	~~8.30 Dentist's appointment~~	9.30 Presentation	8.30 Interview: Ms Jane Morton
		11.00 Interview: Ms Maria Langton		11.00 Dentist's appointment
	2.30 Interview: Mr Peter Marlow	2.00 Interview: Mr S. Rogers	2.30 Visit to MPR Software, Harrow	~~2.00 Interview: Mr S. Rogers~~

WB, pp. 50–53

17 READING WORKING WITH THE TEXT
How to be a teenage millionaire ▸ pp. 44–46 • WB (pp. 71–72)

a) *Put the events of the story (pp. 44–45) in the correct order. Write the numbers 2–8 in the boxes.*

She bought the address whateverlife.com with the money.	3
Ashley started to design websites when she was nine years old.	1
She got her first cheque from an advertising company.	5
Her mother lent her $8 to buy a domain name.	2
Big advertising companies started to get interested in her website.	4
She wants to study design in her dream city, New York.	8
She left school just before her 16th birthday.	6
She had a problem with a friend who was working for her.	7

b) *How would you describe Ashley? What do you know about her? Tick the correct answers.*

1 She's determined and ambitious.	✔	5 She has a strict set of rules for people who work for her.	✔
2 She earns money by selling her designs.		6 She's artistic and hard-working.	✔
3 She doesn't miss school.		7 She lives the normal life of a teenager.	
4 She believes in herself.	✔	8 Her business brings in about $7000 a month.	

WB, pp. 54–58

c) *If Ashley were in your school class, how would you and your classmates feel about it? Would you want to work for her? How would you feel about her strict rules? Write your opinion and explain your arguments. Write in your exercise book.*

2418
2419
I think it would be fun to have a teenage millionaire as a classmate. First, .../I don't think it would be good to work for somebody in your own school class. First, ...

How well can you do these things?	Very well	OK	Practise!
LISTENING AND READING SKILLS: I can …			
… understand longer conversations and stories even if some words are unknown, e.g. *In the outback* (SB pp. 20–23).	☐	☐	☐
… understand and find detailed information from what I hear or read, e.g. details about Ashley Qualls' business (SB pp. 44–45).	☐	☐	☐
… understand the Australian accent without difficulty, e.g. Rob talking about sports (SB p. 13).	☐	☐	☐
SPEAKING AND WRITING SKILLS: I can …			
… start and continue a conversation on an everyday topic with someone I don't know.	☐	☐	☐
… describe my personal qualities and my interests at a job interview.	☐	☐	☐
… write my CV with the correct format and content.	☐	☐	☐
… fill in a job application form.	☐	☐	☐
… write a formal letter of application and a formal letter asking for information in a suitable style and format.	☐	☐	☐
MEDIATION SKILLS: I can …			
… report the most important facts from conversations or written texts, both from German into English and from English into German, e.g. I can talk about English job adverts in German.	☐	☐	☐
… use synonyms or paraphrasing for words and phrases I don't know.	☐	☐	☐
TOPICS: I have learned …			
… about Australia's geography, history, animals, natural sights (e.g. the outback, Uluru, the Great Barrier Reef) and the School of the Air.	☐	☐	☐
… about Aboriginal culture and history, e.g. 'the Dreamtime' and 'the stolen generations'.	☐	☐	☐
… how to talk about jobs, job applications, work experience and qualities needed for different jobs.	☐	☐	☐
… how to call about an interview and ask questions about a job.	☐	☐	☐
… how to present myself at an interview.	☐	☐	☐
STUDY AND LANGUAGE SKILLS: I know …			
… how to understand and talk about bar charts and pie charts.	☐	☐	☐

HOW I COULD IMPROVE[2] MY ENGLISH SKILLS: I could …
(e.g. work through Skills Check 1 again, watch DVDs in English, …)

____

____

____

____

[1] self-evaluation [self ɪˌvælju'eɪʃn] *Selbsteinschätzung* [2] improve [ɪm'pruːv] *verbessern*

Skills Check 2

LISTENING

1 LISTENING First day at work 🎧 11

You are going to hear Jenna talking about her first summer vacation job. First read the sentences, then listen and tick A, B or C. You will hear the recording twice.

1 Jenna got her first summer vacation job in a …
- A clothes store.
- B ✓ shoe store.
- C designer jeans boutique.

2 She wanted to work there because …
- A ✓ she loves shoes.
- B she couldn't get any other job.
- C the store sold shoes for teenagers.

3 Jenna got the job there because …
- A she had work experience.
- B ✓ they needed someone quickly.
- C she was the only applicant[1].

4 The first customer bought shoes in …
- A ✓ brown and black.
- B black and blue.
- C blue and brown.

5 The customer paid … for two pairs of shoes.
- A 155 dollars
- B ✓ 310 dollars
- C 410 dollars

6 Jenna didn't know the correct price because …
- A someone told her the wrong price.
- B ✓ there was no price on the shoes.
- C the price on the box was wrong.

7 When Jenna couldn't find shoes for the second customer, she …
- A asked the manager.
- B showed the customer different shoes.
- C ✓ waited in the store room[2] until the customer had gone.

8 Jenna thought it would be unprofessional to …
- A ✓ say she couldn't find the shoes the customer wanted.
- B ask how the system in the store room worked.
- C hide in the store room.

READING

2 READING Jobs

***a)** Look at the five texts quickly. What are they about? Tick a box.*

Young people describing a job they would like to do. ……………… ☐

Young people describing work experience. ……………… ☐

Young people describing jobs that they do. ……………… ✓

***b)** Read what the five young people say. Look at the pictures on the next page. Which picture matches which description? Write A–F in the boxes. There is one picture more than you need.*

1 [D] I love my job, though it isn't easy. You have to work really hard, and the pay is not good. We work shifts. I often have the night shift, which is quite hard because you're mostly alone, so it's difficult if there's an emergency[3]. I always hope nothing will happen when I'm doing a night shift. We have to know a lot. It's a very responsible job and we mustn't make mistakes. We have to be exact in our work, punctual, reliable, caring and always friendly to our patients.

2 [A] I work outside half of the time. I don't mind because there's usually something going on. And we work in twos on the street, so there's always a partner to talk to. We are often called to a traffic accident, a fight or a robbery in the area. I prefer it to sitting in the office writing up reports, but we have to do that too. There's some routine, but my job is much better than a 9 to 5 job, and it's surprising how much crime there is in a small town. We're always busy. It's never boring.

[1] applicant ['æplɪkənt] *Bewerber/in* [2] store room ['stɔ: ru:m] *Lager* [3] emergency [i'mɜ:dʒənsi] *Notfall*

3 B In my job you have to be calm and organized and you have to be good in a team. I work with my boss and his partner. I always have to be punctual and reliable, but that's no problem. I had to learn a lot and do exams, and I'm still training, so I don't do operations myself yet. It's good that we can help old ladies and children when their pets are ill. But we also help farm animals, cows, sheep, horses. You don't have to mind getting your hands dirty. It's a good feeling being able to help and save lives.

4 F I'm an outdoor person. I definitely couldn't work in an office all day sitting at a desk and looking at a computer. I work for a company in town, but our projects are everywhere in the area, sometimes they're really big projects, office blocks or industrial parks. My job isn't very nice in winter when it's cold and it rains a lot. You have to be fit and quite strong. We carry building materials and we start early. It's nice to look at a beautiful new building and know that you were part of it.

5 E This is my second year of training. It's hard work and I had to start from the bottom, cleaning floors and preparing vegetables – pretty boring. At first I learned all the standard dishes, but I really enjoy being artistic with food and cooking my own dishes. I hope to have my own restaurant one day.

A

Lucy

B
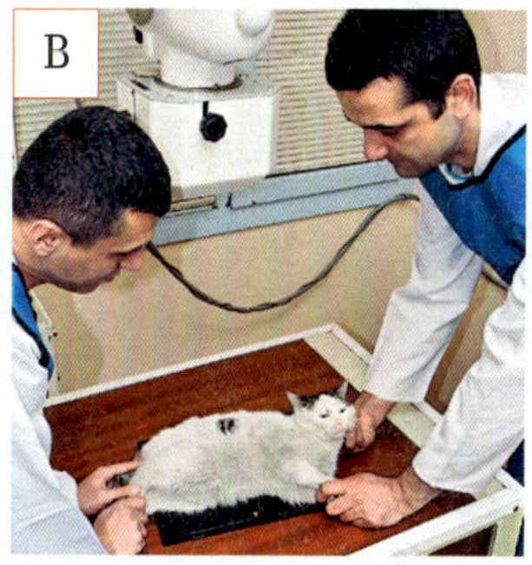
Adam

C

Penny

D
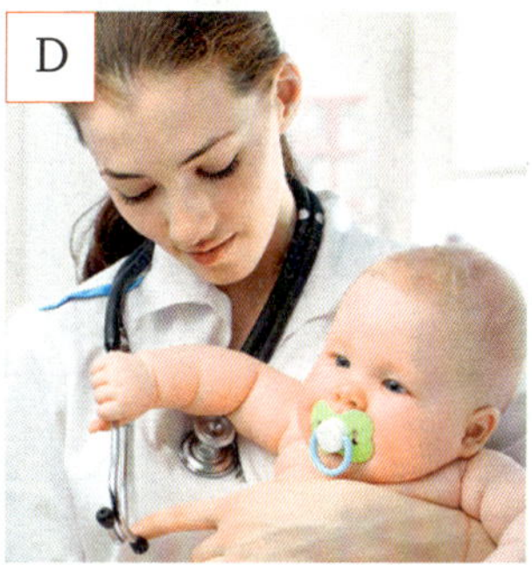
Lauren

E

Nick

F

Sam

c) Write the correct name.

1 Who would like to own his own business? Nick

2 Who likes being part of a big project? Sam

3 Who doesn't like working night shifts? Lauren

4 Who works outdoors about 50%? Lucy

5 Who has finished one year of training? Nick

6 Who assists at operations? Adam

7 Who hates office work? Sam

8 Who has to be fit? Sam

3 WRITING A formal letter

You would like to apply for this summer job in London. Write a formal letter of application to the company. Think about the form and about how to start and end your letter. Write about 80–100 words.

Ferienjob in London?

Wir suchen deutschsprachige Aushilfen für unseren Touristendienst in London (mehrere Stellen) für jeweils 6 bis 8 Wochen in der Zeit von Mai bis September.
Senden Sie bitte Ihre englischsprachigen Bewerbungsunterlagen an:
London Tourist Service
15 Regent Street
London SW1
England

LONDON Tourist Service

4 WRITING Your CV

Now write your CV to send with your application. Which information do you need (personal details, education, qualifications) and in which order? Don't forget a short personal statement.

5 WRITING An informal letter

Write an informal letter to an English friend in London telling him/her about the job in the advert. Say why the job interests you, and write about the good and bad things. Brainstorm your ideas first (mind map, list). Write about 100 words in your exercise book.

SPEAKING

6 SPEAKING Jobs and work experience

a) Look at the two pictures and describe the jobs. Compare their advantages and disadvantages. What are the people doing? How do you think the people feel when they're doing these jobs? Which job would you like? Why? Make notes in English in your exercise book and talk for about two minutes. You can record what you say.

1

2

b) Prepare answers to these questions. Talk for about two minutes. You can record what you say.

- Why do you think work experience is important for young people?
- Talk about your work experience.
- What did you like about it and what didn't you like?
- Do you have a weekend job or an after-school job?
- What kind of job would you like to do when you leave school?

MEDIATION

7 MEDIATION Small ads

You have met an American student. She doesn't speak much German but would like to have a job for a few hours a day. You find some suitable jobs in the local newspaper. Make notes in English in your exercise book first. Then tell her about the jobs.

1 **Café am Brunnen**

Aushilfe gesucht f. ca. 3 Stunden vorm. od. nachm. Arbeiten in Küche und Café (z. B. Gemüse putzen, Küche aufräumen, Tische decken u. abräumen). Servieren von Eis und Kuchen im Gastgarten.
Gute Bezahlung.
Tel.: 793 501

2 **Hotel am Domplatz**

Für unsere Rezeption suchen wir **ab sofort** eine Aushilfe mit sehr guten **Englischkenntnissen.**
Aufgaben: telefonische Auskunft u. Betreuung ausländischer Gäste.
Erfahrung in der Hotelbranche erwünscht, aber nicht Voraussetzung.
Halbtags od. stundenweise.
Überdurchschnittliche Bezahlung.
Tel.: 482 502 (Fr. Lenz)

3 **Englischsprachige Kinderbetreuung**

für amerikanische Familie gesucht (Kinder 2 u. 4 J.).
Mo–Fr, 13–17 Uhr. Keine Arbeit im Haushalt.
Führerschein nicht erforderlich.
Tel.: 602 335

4 Student/in für **englische Konversation** gesucht. Mo u. Do vorm. je 2 St. (Gruppe 6 Pers.), 2. Gruppe Di u. Fr möglich, **native speaker** willkommen! Deutschkenntnisse nicht erforderlich. Tel.: 496 395 (Vera)

Well, there's a job in a café. You have to ...

How did you do?

Check your answers to the exercises on p. 80. Then answer the questions below with Yes or No. If you tick No or would like some extra practice on that point, go to the exercise in your workbook (pp. 50–70).

	Yes	No	Exercise
1 LISTENING First day at work			
1 Konntest du nach dem 1. Hören beurteilen, um was es im Wesentlichen geht?	☐	☐	1, 2, 9a
2 Hast du dir beim 1. Hören Angaben zu Zahlen und Details notiert?	☐	☐	3, 5
3 Konntest du den amerikanischen Akzent erkennen und mühelos verstehen?	☐	☐	6, 7, 9
4 Konntest du dem Sprechtempo problemlos folgen?	☐	☐	8
2 READING Jobs			
1 Konntest du schnell herausfinden, um was es jeweils in den Texten geht?	☐	☐	10, 16a
2 Konntest du Antworten auf Detailfragen problemlos finden?	☐	☐	13, 14
3 Hast du die Bedeutung unbekannter Wörter erschließen können?	☐	☐	15, 16b
3 WRITING A formal letter			
1 Hast du genau gewusst, wie die äußere Form eines *formal letter* aussieht?	☐	☐	20b
2 Hast du eine höfliche Anrede und passende Schlussformel benutzt?	☐	☐	20a
3 Hast du deine Rechtschreibung/Grammatik überprüft und deine Fehler korrigiert?	☐	☐	35
4 WRITING Your CV			
1 Hast du alle erforderlichen Informationen in der richtigen Reihenfolge präsentiert?	☐	☐	21a+c
2 Ist es dir leicht gefallen, ein kurzes, treffendes *personal statement* zu schreiben?	☐	☐	21b
5 WRITING An informal letter			
1 Hast du eine passende Gruß- und Schlussformel benutzt?	☐	☐	17b
2 Hast du versucht, mithilfe eines *brainstorming* Ideen zu sammeln?	☐	☐	17a
6 SPEAKING Jobs and work experience			
1 Hast du mit dem *present progressive* (z.B. *is telling*) beschrieben, was die Personen auf den Bildern gerade tun?	☐	☐	28
2 Hast du die Jobs mit passenden Adjektiven (z.B. *hard, good*) beschrieben?	☐	☐	33
3 Hast du wichtige Vokabeln für die Bildbeschreibung (z.B. *in the background* usw.) gewusst?	☐	☐	23a, 24 a+b
4 Hast du problemlos deine Meinung zu den Fragen ausdrücken können?	☐	☐	23b
5 Hast du über deine *work experience* im *simple past* (z.B. *worked*) erzählt?	☐	☐	29
7 MEDIATION Small ads			
1 Hast du beachtet, mit eigenen Worten nur das Wesentliche weiterzugeben bzw. nicht alles wörtlich zu übersetzen?	☐	☐	25, 26
2 Hast du (falls nötig) für unbekannte Wörter Umschreibungen benutzt (*paraphrasing*)?	☐	☐	32
3 Hast du modale Hilfsverben richtig benutzt (*can, have to, needn't* usw.)?	☐	☐	27

Unit 3 Teen world

1 Hannah, Craig and Lina ▸ pp. 48–49

a) Read pp. 48–49 of your student's book again. Are the statements below true or false? Mark a letter.

		True	False
1	Lina comes from the UK.	O	E
2	Hannah is very interested in fashion.	I	G
3	Lina isn't good at science subjects in school.	N	A
4	Craig has a summer job.	G	E
5	Lina works hard at school and at home.	R	P
6	Craig would love to have a career in a bank.	S	N
7	Hannah spends hours on the phone.	I	R

b) If your answers are correct, in the right order the letters you have marked spell the name of a country:

Nigeria.

c) Who would you like to have as a friend: Hannah, Craig or Lina? Say why. First make notes. Then write a paragraph in your exercise book. Ideas:

hard-working • fun • sporty • ambitious • determined • popular • interested in … • good at … • organized

2 STUDY SKILLS Outline and written discussion ▸ p. 51 • SF (p. 140)

Find arguments for and against this statement:

School students should not be allowed to have a TV in their room.

Add arguments and points to the following outline and write your complete text in your exercise book.

1	Introduction	Almost all school students watch TV in the evening, but should they have a TV in their room? …
2	First point of view	Some people think that school students should have their own TV …
2.1	First argument	First, young people don't always want to see the same programmes as their parents …
2.2	Second argument	…
2.3	…	…
3	Opposite point of view	However, is it really a good idea for school students to watch TV when they want and as long as they want? …
3.1	First argument	Young people maybe watch programmes that are bad or not suitable, for example …
3.2	…	Another argument is that …
3.3	…	Third, …
4	Conclusion	After looking at both sides, I think that …

3 WORDS Get it right! (False friends) ▸ p. 52

a) What's wrong with Lisa's e-mail to her British friend? Underline seven more mistakes and write what's correct.

E-mail

Last week my little brother and I both became a new mobile. My parents are quite strong, so they told us not to make unnecessary calls. My brother is brave, so he doesn't use his mobile as much as me. For example, when I want to talk to a friend in the evening, I don't usually call from my parents' phone in the floor, I just use my mobile. Dad sometimes tells me not to chat so much, but in my meaning that's OK. Dad pays our bills[1], so he's the chef. I promised him I would try really hard to get better notes in Maths and English. Than he was happy.

got
strict
good
hall
opinion
boss
marks/grades, Then

INFO BOX

In Germany 92 % of young people aged 12 to 19 have a mobile phone, 69 % of kids from 10 to 13, 16 % of kids under 10!
Half of the kids pay part of their monthly mobile bill. 20 % of the kids pay the bill themselves!
(Source: KidsVA 2009, Egmont Ehapa Verlag)

b) First match the English words to their German meanings. Then use the English word in a sentence. Write in your exercise book.

floor meaning cake become than strong note

3303 Kuchen werden Fußboden als Notiz Bedeutung stark

4 EVERYDAY ENGLISH Mobiles ▸ p. 52

a) Match the verbs with words from the box. Sometimes there's more than one.

a call • your mailbox • a message • a phone number • a photo • a ringtone • the time

1 check your mailbox, the time, ...
2 download a ringtone, a photo
3 miss a call
4 save a phone number, a message
5 make a call
6 take a photo, a call, a message, ...
7 text a message
8 receive/get a call, a message

b) Now complete what Latika says about how she uses her mobile with phrases from a).

I make most calls at the weekend. I text five messages a day on average and I often check my mailbox. I always save phone numbers of new contacts. I don't often take photos, but sometimes I download a new ringtone. I receive/get a few text messages from friends, but I don't always read them till later. If I miss a call I usually phone back, but not always. Oh, and I don't need a watch any more. I use my mobile to check the time or set an

3304 alarm[2]. My mobile makes life easier, but I'm never its slave!

[1] bill [bɪl] *Rechnung* [2] alarm [əˈlɑːm] *Wecker*

5 ENGLISH FOR JOBS Useful job phrases ▸ p. 53

*a) Who says what? Write **C** (customer) or **A** (shop assistant).*

Can I help you? A
There's your receipt. A
I'd like .../I'm looking for ... C
Here's your change. A
Do you want to pay cash or by credit card? A
This one's a bit more expensive. A
3405 Have you got this/these in other colours/sizes? C

I'll take this/these, please. C
Would you like anything else? A
That's ... euros/pounds, please. A
I'm just looking first, thank you. C
Just a moment. I'll check. A
These are very popular. A
Where's the lift, please? C

b) In your exercise book, write a dialogue between the shop assistant and the customer. Decide what the customer wants to buy, for example a sports bag or an MP3 player. Use as many phrases from a) as you can.

6 Teens in trouble ▸ p. 55

a) Choose some of the words from the box in the correct form to complete the sentences below.

attack • ban • behaviour • cause • court • fights • kick • law • motorbikes • offer • order
orphan • police • punishment • straighten up • vandalize

1 The 'B' in 'ASBO' means 'behaviour'.
2 The 'O' in 'ASBO' means 'order'.
3 Shane was given a four-year ASBO by the court.
4 He caused serious trouble many times.
3406 5 He kicked footballs against houses and cars.
6 He rode motorbikes on the pavement.
7 He attacked other teenagers.
8 He was banned from some areas of town.
9 The ASBO was his punishment.
10 It helped him to straighten up his life.

b) Shane is now 17 and doing well. How do you think he feels about himself and about his future? Write about six sentences in your exercise book. Ideas:

feels proud of himself • serious about work • looking forward to his future • job and money

Now you ▸ SF (p. 137)

Do you think that an ASBO is a good way to stop anti-social behaviour? Write a formal letter to a magazine and give reasons for your opinion. Read pp. 54–55 of your student's book again first. Use your exercise book or a computer. Ideas:

have nothing to do • no job • no money • feel bored and angry • don't care • need 'fun'

Dear Sir or Madam
I would like to share my opinion on anti-social behaviour and teenagers with readers of your magazine.
First, ... Second, ...

7 SPEAKING COURSE Part 3: Discussion phrases (Having a discussion)

▸ p. 56 • WB (p. 75) 🎧 12, 13

a) Tick the correct phrase. During a discussion, what would you say …

1 … when you want to know someone's opinion?

A I see what you mean. | B ✓ What do you think? | C Could you say that again, please?

2 … when you want to say what you think?

A I agree with you. | B No, that's not right. | C ✓ In my opinion, …

3 … when you think/feel the same as the speaker?

A Could you say that again? | B ✓ I agree with you. | C Let me explain.

4 … when you want to say that you understand the speaker's point?

A ✓ I see what you mean. | B Wait a minute. Let me finish. | C Sorry, I don't agree with you.

5 … when you are speaking and someone else starts to speak?

A No, that's not right. | B Could you say that again, please? | C ✓ Wait a minute. Let me finish.

6 … when you don't think/feel the same as the speaker?

A I know you're right. | B ✓ Sorry, I don't agree with you. | C That's true.

7 … when you think what someone said is wrong?

A I don't understand what you mean. | B You're right. | C ✓ No, that's not right.

b) Read the discussion phrases below. Then listen (🎧 12) to Guy, Mel and Ali, three UK teenagers, who are talking about ASBOs. Write down the order that you hear the discussion phrases in (2–11).

I agree with you. (5)
In my opinion, … (1)
Wait a minute. Let me finish. (2)
What do you think? (4)
First, … (7)
Second, … (8)
That's a good point. (3)
I see what you mean. (9)
Sorry, but I don't agree with you. (6)
No, that's not right. (10)
That's true. (11)

c) Listen again (🎧 13) to the discussion and in the pauses fill in the missing phrases. Do this exercise at least twice.

/B, pp. 3–64

3507

8 WORDS Boot camps ▸ p. 56

Look at p. 55 of your student's book again and complete the text about boot camps with suitable words/phrases.

In the USA teenagers in trouble can volunteer to go to a boot camp instead of *prison*. Young people who have *committed* a crime go to a boot camp to *straighten up their lives* and learn *discipline*. They have to get up very early and do lots of sport, so they can *get fit*. That's a good thing. But life at a boot camp, which is a *military*-style school, is very hard. The teenagers must *follow* rules even if the rules are stupid. The drill *instructors* are very strict. They give lots of *punishments* if the boys do not follow their *orders* exactly. Boot
3608 camp isn't a game – and it really isn't fun.

9 Blue box: hard-working, warm-hearted ▸ p. 57, p. 170

Describe yourself and a friend. Make suitable adjectives from the boxes to complete the sentences. Write the sentences in your exercise book.

1 I am *fun-loving …*
2 I'm not *time-wasting …*
3 My best friend/boyfriend/girlfriend is …
4 My best friend/boyfriend/girlfriend isn't …

3609

1	2
fun- • hard- • music- • nature- • good- • quick- • time- • warm- • well-	behaved • dressed • hearted • looking • loving • organized • thinking • wasting • working

10 WORDS Adjectives: 'interested' or 'interesting'? ▸ p. 57

a) *Find matching pairs.*

interesting	gelangweilt	excited	überrascht
bored	interessant	surprised	verblüfft
shocking	schockiert	amazing	aufgeregt
boring	interessiert	surprising	verblüffend
interested	schockierend	exciting	aufregend
shocked	langweilig	amazed	überraschend

b) *Complete what Rick says with words from a).*

We watched a scary film last night. It was quite *exciting* (excite) at first. In the middle I got a bit *bored* (bore) because the story wasn't really *interesting* (interest). But the special effects were *amazing* (amaze). My sister looked quite *shocked* (shock) because the cybermonsters were so ugly. Of course the end wasn't *surprising* (surprise). It was really stupid. But my sister didn't seem to find the story *boring* (bore). Just imagine, after the film was over, she said she was *surprised* (surprise) that I watched that rubbish! I'm sure she enjoyed the film more
3610 than me!

11 Kids getting into trouble (Understanding participle clauses) ▸ p. 57 • WB (p. 77)

a) *Which sentences contain a participle clause? Underline the clauses.*

1 The girl driving the car didn't have a licence.

2 Teenagers committing crimes maybe need help instead of punishment.

3 My dad saw a boy with a gun while he was driving past the old factory in Hill Street.

4 The kids spraying graffiti were about 13 years old.

5 Some neighbours saw two youths vandalizing a children's play area.

6 People are moving away from our area of town because of trouble-makers.

3711 ***b)*** *Translate the clauses you have underlined into German. Write in your exercise book.*

12 REVISION Volunteer work (Passive: simple present/simple past) ▸ p. 60 • WB (p. 78)

Complete what Tess says about volunteer work with the verbs in brackets in the passive, simple present or simple past.

Young people *are needed* to do volunteer work in over a hundred countries.

Hi, my name's Tess. Young people *are needed* (need) to do volunteer work in over a hundred countries. People always ask me what kind of work *is done* (do) by volunteers. Well, everything! For example, buildings *are repaired* (repair), nature *is protected* (protect), children and sick people *are helped* (help), English *is taught* (teach). Last year I was in a small village called Onwe, near Kumasi in Ghana. During my four weeks there the school room *was repaired* (repair) and a children's play area *was built* (build), and thanks to a new project a small lake in the area *was cleaned up* (clean up). Volunteering is great. You know that you are giving help where

3712 it *is really needed* (really, need).

13 So much has been done (Passive: present perfect) ▸ p. 60 • WB (p. 78)

A group of young volunteers has been helping with a project at a village school in Cameroon. This is what **has/hasn't been done** *so far. Complete the sentences with the present perfect passive.*

1 The school building *has been painted* (paint).

2 A new classroom *has been added* (add).

3 A fence *hasn't been built* (not build).

4 Trees *have been planted* (plant).

5 The computers *haven't been installed yet* (not install, yet).

3713 6 Toilets *have been put in* (put in).

14 Volunteering in India (Passive: will-future, modals)

► p. 61 • WB (p. 78)

An international group of young volunteers has arrived in a village near Kolkata, India. The project leader of the international work camp welcomes the volunteers and gives them general information. Complete some of the things he says with sentences in the passive.

1 You will be divided (will – divide) into work groups of four students.

2 A list of names will be put up (will – put up) on the notice board in the main building.

3 Camp rules should be followed (should – follow).

4 The camp must be kept (must – keep) as clean and tidy as possible.

5 Local traditions must be respected (must – respect) at all times.

6 Alcohol must not be brought (must not – bring) into the camp.

7 All instructions will be given (will – give) in English by your group leaders.

8 Any problems should be reported (should – report) to the group leaders.

9 Changes can be made (can – make) to your programme if you're not happy.

3814 10 The project leader should be called (should – call) if you're ill and need a doctor.

15 MEDIATION International work camps

► p. 61 • WB (p. 76)

Tell a British exchange student the main facts from the following website information: who takes part in the work camp programmes, how long you stay, what kind of work you do, how long you work, free time activities, etc. Make notes in English in your exercise book first.

Internationale Workcamps für Teenager

Wer, wo und wann?
Jedes Jahr nehmen junge Leute aus aller Welt an Hilfsprojekten in internationalen Workcamps in über hundert Ländern teil. Dabei lernen die Teilnehmer/innen nicht nur andere Länder und Kulturen kennen. Bei einem Aufenthalt von zwei bis sechs Wochen arbeiten sie zusammen an einem sinnvollen Projekt. Die Camps finden meist in den Monaten Juni bis September für die Altersgruppen von 14 bis 19 Jahren statt.

Arbeitsgruppen und Arbeitsbereiche
In jeder Workcamp-Gruppe sind 10 bis höchstens 20 Teilnehmer/innen, die jeden Tag ca. vier Stunden mit einem Gruppenleiter/einer Gruppenleiterin zusammen arbeiten. Die Arbeitsbereiche sind vielfältig, z.B. Umweltprojekte, die Betreuung von Kindern, Englischunterricht, Mitarbeit in Krankenhäusern oder Waisenhäusern, die Renovierung von Schulen, Jugendzentren und Spielplätzen oder historischen Gebäuden. Die Campsprache ist meist Englisch.

Unterbringung und Freizeit
Unterkünfte, z.B. in Jugendzentren oder Jugendherbergen werden zur Verfügung gestellt. Auch die Verpflegung ist kostenfrei. Oft wird nicht nur zusammen gegessen, sondern unter Anleitung auch zusammen gekocht. Freizeitaktivitäten kommen auch nicht zu kurz. Zum Freizeitprogramm gehören nicht nur gemeinsame Ausflüge und Sightseeing, sondern auch Workshops. Viel Sport sowie Fahrradtouren und Wanderungen gehören auch dazu.

WB, pp. 65–66

16 READING WORKING WITH THE TEXT The caller

▸ pp. 62–64 • WB (pp. 71–72)

a) *How well do you know the story (student's book pp. 62–64)? Read the summary carefully. Some details are not correct. Mark wrong sentences, sentence parts or words.*

Lindsay's Aunt Margaret has died. At the funeral Lindsay's dad can't find his car keys. Later at home, when Lindsay gets a call from a voice that says it's Aunt Margaret, she thinks it's her friend Candice who is playing a trick on her. Lindsay goes to Missy's party and wears Aunt Margaret's gold earrings to make the other girls jealous. When the voice of Aunt Margaret calls Lindsay again from her father's cellphone, Lindsay thinks it's her cousins who are playing a trick. Lindsay tells the voice that she was only nice to her because she wanted her earrings. That evening all the girls stay at Missy's house. Lindsay gets a third call from the unknown caller from her father's cellphone. The voice says she's coming back to get the earrings. Lindsay thinks it's her brothers again who have found the phone and are trying to trick her. Lindsay calls home, but her mom says the boys are playing cards. In the middle of the call the lights go out at Lindsay's house and there's a loud noise. Then someone knocks at the back door of Missy's house. Lindsay is scared. She wants Missy to look who is at the door. Missy leaves Lindsay alone upstairs. Then Lindsay's phone rings again. She hears a knock on the window and is afraid that it's Aunt Margaret's ghost[1]. The voice in the next room sounds like Missy's, laughing at Lindsay because she's crying like a baby. Angry with Missy, Lindsay opens the door, but it is not Missy who is holding the phone in a muddy[2] hand …

b) *Find at least two parts in the story that show the reader something about Lindsay's character. Give the line numbers and say what the reader learns about Lindsay.*

1) ll. 5–7: Lindsay doesn't want to be at the funeral. She wants to get ready for her friend's party. This shows that Lindsay isn't sad and that she has no real feelings for Aunt Margaret.

2) ll. 52–59: When Lindsay is ready to go to Missy's party, she takes Aunt Margaret's gold ring, because she wants to show off at the party.

c) *Some things happen in the story that can't be explained in a logical way. Find examples of this in the text and summarize them in your own words.*

Lindsay's father loses his mobile at the funeral. Lindsay knows that someone is using it, but it isn't her family and it isn't Missy. She gets a call from a voice that says that she is Aunt Margaret and wants to take the ring back because Lindsay doesn't deserve it. At the end of the story it isn't clear who the caller is …

d) *What makes a good scary story? Think about a scary film you have seen or a scary book you have read. Write notes and discuss your ideas in class.*

a strange person or strange people, a lonely place, a strange situation, noises in the night, things or people disappear …

WB, pp. 54–58
3917
3918

[1] ghost [gəʊst] *Geist* [2] muddy ['mʌdɪ] *schlammverschmiert*

Unit 4 Big city life

1 Describing a picture ▸ pp. 74–75 • SF (p. 121)

Choose one of the pictures on p. 74 or 75 of your student's book and describe it in detail. First, say what the picture shows. Then say where you can see what. Describe the people and the building(s).

The picture that I have chosen shows a street scene in .../a very poor area in ... I think the picture was taken in the evening/afternoon. In the foreground/middle/ ... you can see ... On the left/right there's/ ...

2 Mumbai, India: What do you know? ▸ p. 78

Test

a) *Choose the correct answer. Tick A, B or C. You need the letters in brackets in b).*

1 The capital of India is ...

A Mumbai. (A)	B ✓ New Delhi. (H)	C Bombay. (R)

2 In which year did Bombay get its new name 'Mumbai'?

A In 1661. (J)	B In 1947. (O)	C ✓ In 1996. (A)

3 For almost 300 years, India was under British control. This is ...

A ✓ true. (G)	B false. (A)	C not given in the text. (R)

4 Bollywood is ...

A Mumbai's financial centre. (P)	B ✓ the name of India's film industry. (D)	C a tourist theme park. (U)

5 What is Marathi?

A ✓ An Indian language. (N)	B A Mumbai slum. (U)	C Mumbai's financial centre. (R)

6 Which language is used most for business and in offices?

A Hindi. (G)	B Gujarati. (B)	C ✓ English. (I)

b) *Now write the letters in brackets from a) in the boxes below. The letters make the name of a famous person:*

3	2	5	4	1	6
G	A	N	D	H	I

c) **Extra** *Do research on Mahatma Gandhi. Find out five important facts to present in class.*

INFO BOX

In Mumbai there is a great contrast between rich and poor. A large percentage of Mumbai's population live in slums, in very poor quality homes or on the streets.
By contrast, the richest people in India live in Mumbai. The city is the home of 23 billionaires!

3 WORDS Describing things and places in the city ▸ p. 79

a) Which words do not fit? First underline the adjectives that you would not generally use to describe the nouns given. Then add two suitable adjectives to each list.

1 **skyscrapers:** shiny, stressed, huge, tall, modern

2 **shopping malls:** expensive, fashionable, busy, polluted, popular, crowded

3 **the public transport system:** crowded, clean, financial, cheap, reliable, fast

4 **financial centres:** international, colourful, world-famous, modern, busy, important

5 **suburbs:** poor, rich, modern, crowded, shiny, clean, quiet, safe, noisy

b) Write sentences about Mumbai from the information on pp. 76–78 of your student's book. Use suitable adjective and noun combinations from a).

1 There are lots of shiny, modern skyscrapers in Mumbai.

2 There are some very expensive and fashionable shopping malls in the rich parts of Mumbai.

3 There is a cheap but crowded public transport system in Mumbai.

4 Mumbai is India's most important international financial centre.

4103
4104 5 There are poor and crowded suburbs in Mumbai.

4 REVISION If I went to Mumbai, ... (Conditional sentences II) ▸ p. 79 • WB (p. 78)

Imagine what you would do and what you wouldn't do if you went to Mumbai. Complete the sentences with **would**, **could** *or* **might**. *You can use ideas from the box or your own ideas.*

1 If I went to Mumbai, I would/could/might ______

2 If I had (have) enough money, I ______

3 If I had (have) enough time, I ______

- learn about India's history
- take a ride in an auto-rickshaw
- do a Bollywood studios tour
- take an elephant ride
- do volunteer work in the villages
- watch a Bollywood film
- enjoy the delicious food
- take a bus tour of the city
- buy some things at the street markets

4105

5 Johannesburg: What do you know? ▸ p. 81

a) Are the statements true or false? Mark a letter.

	True	False
1 A short, popular name for Johannesburg is 'Joburg'.	F	A
2 Johannesburg is the capital of South Africa.	U	A
3 Johannesburg is not South Africa's largest city.	J	N
4 During apartheid, blacks were not allowed to live in the same areas as whites.	K	R
5 Soweto means 'South West Territory'.	T	A
6 The townships were the result of strict racial segregation laws in 1910.	P	R
7 When apartheid ended, black people were allowed to vote.	A	O
8 Nelson Mandela was elected first black president of South Africa in 1994.	S	A
9 Today Johannesburg has a high crime rate.	I	F

b) If the letters you have marked are correct, in the right order they spell the name of a language:

AFRIKAANS.

6 READING WORKING WITH THE TEXT A tour of Soweto ▸ pp. 81–82 • WB (pp. 71–72)

a) Read the story on pp. 81–82 of your student's book again. What does the text tell the reader about Soweto? List some facts, for example who lives there, facts about Soweto's history and how people live. Give the line numbers and make notes.

ll. 5–7: only black people live in Soweto

ll. 11–13: one third of the babies born there have AIDS

ll. 15–18: two Nobel Peace Prize winners

ll. 29–30: schoolchildren shot during uprising in 1976

ll. 31–43: people live in terrible shacks

ll. 47–51: people of Soweto want tourists to see what life is like there

WB, pp. 54–58

b) Use your notes from a) to write a short text about Soweto in your own words. Add important facts. Your facts need not be in the same order as in the story. Write in your exercise book.

'Soweto' is the short name for the 'South West township' of Johannesburg. Only black people live there ...

● *c)* **Extra** *What do you think Berry wrote in her diary after her visit to Soweto? Use the ideas below or your own ideas. Write a paragraph in your exercise book.*

Today Dad and I did a tour of Soweto. A man called Mr Otambo drove us through some of the neighbourhoods in his car. I learned a lot and saw a lot – not all good. I felt ...

7 MEDIATION Too much sun ▸ p. 84 • WB (p. 76)

a) Read the questions below first, then scan the text to find the answers. Which questions does the text answer? Tick them (✔). Which questions does the text not answer? Cross them (✘).

1 Wann sollte man eine Sonnencreme benutzen? ✔
2 Wann sollte man nicht in die Sonne gehen? ✔
3 Was ist beim Schwimmen zu beachten? ✔
4 Wie oft sollte man eine Sonnencreme auftragen? ✘
5 Was ist bei Kindern zu beachten? ✔
6 Wie viel Wasser sollte man in der Sonne trinken? ✘

PROTECTING YOUR BODY FROM SUNBURN

When you're travelling in a hot country, one of your problems could be too much sun. When your skin starts to hurt, it's usually too late. But there are a few things you can do to protect yourself.

Sunscreen
Use sunscreen at least half an hour before you go in the sun. If the sun is very strong, use an SPF[1] 30. This is a must for children.

Choose the right time to sunbathe
Don't go in the sun at the hottest times of the day, usually between 11 am and 3 pm. Don't sit in the direct sun. Sit under a tree or umbrella.

Sun and water
Wear a T-shirt when you go in the water. This is also a must for children. After swimming in the sea, if possible take a shower to wash off the salt water, which dries your skin. Don't forget to use sunscreen again after your swim.

Which clothes to wear in the sun
When you're outdoors but not on a beach, wear long trousers, a cap or a hat and sunglasses. Cover your arms and shoulders. White and light colours are more suitable than black and dark colours.

WB, pp. 65–66

b) Tell a German friend the answers to the questions.

8 WORDS Tricky words (German 'machen') ▸ p. 84

a) Match the words that go together. Write lists.

be	... fun, on holiday, on a trip
do	... business, an exercise, homework, a project, tricks
go	... for a walk, on a trip, ...
make	... a cake, a mistake, your bed, ...
take	... a break, notes, photos, ...

... a break	... a mistake
... business	... notes
... a cake	... on holiday
... an exercise	... on a trip
... for a walk	... photos
... fun	... a project
... homework	... tricks
... your bed	

b) Translate the sentences into English. Think carefully how to translate 'machen'.

1 Ich habe gerade eine englische Übung gemacht. I've just done an English exercise.
2 Ich habe keine Fehler gemacht. I haven't made any mistakes.
3 Ich werde jetzt eine kurze Pause machen. I'm going to take a short break now.
4 Ich möchte einen Spaziergang machen. I'd like to go for a walk.
4308 5 Englischlernen macht Spaß – nicht wahr? Learning English is fun – isn't it?

[1] Sun Protection Factor [prəˈtekʃn fæktə] *Sonnenschutzfaktor*

9 Tony would have done something else (Conditional sentences III)

▸ p. 84 • WB (p. 78)

*Tony went to Johannesburg with some friends. They did everything together, but Tony **would have done** some things differently. Where **would** he **have gone**? What **would** he **have done**?*

1 On the first day they went shopping. (go sightseeing)

Tony would have gone sightseeing.

2 On the first evening they went to a disco. (watch TV)

Tony would have watched TV.

3 On the second day they did a walking tour. (do a bus tour)

Tony would have done a bus tour.

4 In the evenings they always ate at a pizza place. (prefer South African food)

Tony would have preferred South African food.

5 On the last day of their trip they visited the zoo. (visit the Apartheid Museum)

4409

Tony would have visited the Apartheid Museum.

Now you

*If you had been in Johannesburg with Tony and his friends, which of the things above **would** you **have done**? Write three more sentences in your exercise book.*

I think I would have visited the Apartheid Museum too.
I don't think I would have ...

INFO BOX

Johannesburg is one of the world's most important business centres for gold. Almost half the world's gold is found in the area.
Johannesburg is also very green. People say there are more than 10 million trees in and around the city!

10 ENGLISH FOR JOBS WRITING A letter of enquiry

▸ p. 85 • SF (p. 137)

You are doing an apprenticeship at a German travel agency. Your boss asks you to write an e-mail in English to a tour company in Johannesburg. You have to find out about safari tours to Kruger National Park. You should ask about these things:

- how many days the different tours last
- where people could stay
- how big the tour groups are
- if any of the tours are suitable for persons in wheelchairs
- if any of the tours are suitable for children (over eight years of age)
- prices, services and programme details.

Write a formal letter. Use:

- a subject line
- a suitable beginning
- two or three short paragraphs
- a suitable last sentence
- a formal ending.

WB, pp. 59–62

Use the letter on p. 85 of your student's book for help.
Write your letter in your exercise book or on the computer.

XL Travel Agency
Paulstrasse 2
10435 Berlin
Germany
...
TOP Tours
35 John Street
2123 Johannesburg
South Africa

Enquiry about ...

Dear ...
I am writing to ...
...
...
...
Yours ...

11 WORDS Adjectives ▸ p. 89

a) In your exercise book, make lists of adjectives with the endings -y, -less, -ful and -able. How many do you know? You can use your Dictionary on pp. 177–212 of your student's book for help.

-y	-less	-ful	-able
cloudy	cloudless	beautiful	reliable

b) Katie is in Germany with a group of students. Complete part of her e-mail to a friend in the UK. Add the endings -y, -less, -ful or -able to make suitable adjectives from the words in brackets. Be careful, you have to use un- with two adjectives.

Hi Ava!

We're in Berlin and it's so cool! The people are friendly and really helpful (help) when you ask them things. I'm not very successful (success) with German, but most people here speak English 😊.

The Fall of the Wall must have been an unforgettable (forget) experience for the people in both parts of the city. The shopping malls here are unbelievable (believe), so trendy. We've seen some cool and fashionable (fashion) areas of the city, but we've seen a lot of homeless (home) people living on the streets and under bridges too. We've been quite lucky (luck) with the weather. It's been rainy (rain) some of the time, but if you wear suitable (suit) clothes – like rubber boots[1]! – that's no problem.

4511 Not much sun, but then too much sun isn't healthy (health)!

12 EVERYDAY ENGLISH At a hotel ▸ p. 89 🎧 14

a) Match the receptionist's sentences to the situations below. Write in your exercise book.

Hello. Can I help you? • Breakfast is served from 7 to 11 am. • Did you book a single or a double room? • How would you like to pay? • Would you fill in this form, please? • Here's your key card, sir/madam. • The breakfast room is on the first floor. • Did you have any extras from room service? • The lifts are over there on the right. • I hope you enjoyed your stay. • The price includes breakfast.

1 Checking in	2 Checking out	3 Giving information
Hello. Can I help you?	...	...

4512 4513

b) In your exercise book, write a dialogue between the receptionist and a hotel guest who is checking in. Use suitable phrases from a). Then listen to your CD (🎧 14) and check. Is your text similar to the suggested dialogue?

[1] rubber boots *Gummistiefel*

13 WORDS Words with a similar meaning ▸ p. 89

a) Find words in the box with a similar meaning and write pairs.

connect: link — similar to: like

maybe: perhaps — complete: finish

sum up: summarize — difference: contrast

immediately: at once — talk about: discuss

mostly: mainly — find: discover

at once • contrast • discover • discuss • finish • like • link • mainly • perhaps • summarize

b) Underline the word in each sentence that you can change. Then use a word from a) with a similar meaning.

1 We talked about the history of apartheid in school today. discussed

2 Gold was found in South Africa in 1885. discovered

3 The population of Johannesburg is mostly black African. mainly

4 The difference between rich and poor people is shocking. contrast

5 Maybe I'll do a presentation about Johannesburg. Perhaps

4613 6 At the end of your talk, don't forget to summarize your main points. sum up

14 WORDS Unit 4 puzzle ▸ p. 89

Write the answers in the puzzle and find the word in the orange boxes.

1 There are 11 … languages in South Africa. — 1 official

2 The opposite of 'war' is … — 2 peace

3 The old name for Mumbai is … — 3 Bombay

4 The … of the Mumbai trains are very crowded. — 4 carriages

5 Someone who travels to work in the city every day. — 5 commuter

6 One of the main languages in Mumbai is … — 6 Hindi

7 The two Germanies were … in 1990. — 7 reunified

8 The 'Soweto …' took place on 16th June, 1976. — 8 uprising

4614 9 This tells you about places to visit and things to do in a big city. — 9 guidebook

15 LISTENING Calling reception

▸ p. 89 • WB (p. 71) 🎧 15

Listen to the telephone calls between the hotel receptionist and three hotel guests. What do the guests want? Tick the correct box. More than one answer may be correct.

VB, pp.
0–53

Guest 1:	room service		a different room	✔	check out early	
Guest 2:	help with bags	✔	flight information		a taxi to the airport	✔
Guest 3:	check out early	✔	breakfast in his room		a wake-up call	✔

INFO BOX

Berlin is ...
- nine times bigger than Paris.
- home of the largest department store in Europe, the KaDeWe (Kaufhaus des Westens).

Berlin has ...
- 150 theatres and concert halls.
- 170 museums.
- the biggest zoo in the world with more than 14,000 animals.

16 STUDY SKILLS Visual materials

▸ p. 89 • SF (p. 125)

a) *How many visual materials do you know? Write a list.*

pictures, photos, maps, timelines, posters, transparencies, charts, slides

b) *Why is it good to use visual materials in your presentations?*

They make your presentation more interesting and easier to understand and listen to. Your listeners can imagine the things/places in your talk better. Charts help listeners to understand figures and percentages better.

c) *Make a pie chart which you could use in a presentation on Johannesburg. For example, the chart could show the different ethnic groups in the city.*

Ethnic groups:

- ☐ 73% Blacks
- ☐ 16% Whites
- ☐ 6% Other
- ☐ 4% Asians

d) *What phrases can you use in your presentation to talk about charts?*

Here is a pie/bar chart of ... It shows that ... You can see that ... From the chart it is also clear that ...

17 SPEAKING COURSE Part 4: A talk about Johannesburg (Giving a presentation)

▸ p. 90 • WB (p. 75)

a) Use the sentences for a short presentation about Johannesburg. First, put them in the correct order 2–9.

To sum up my talk: we have seen that Johannesburg is a city of great contrasts with an interesting history.	7
My topic today is 'Johannesburg: past and present'.	1
Would anybody like to ask questions or make comments?	8
After that I'd like to look at the history of Johannesburg.	4
I have divided my presentation into four sections.	2
Finally, I'd like to present some slides of typical city sights.	6
In the third section I'll describe the city's present problems.	5
I'll begin with some general facts about the city's population, etc.	3
If there are no more questions, I'd like to thank you for listening.	9

WB, pp. 63–64

b) In your exercise book, prepare a paragraph for each of your three main sections: 1) general facts, 2) Johannesburg's history, 3) the city's present problems. You can use information from p. 81 of your student's book, include material from exercise 16 (WB p. 47) or do your own research. Give your presentation in class.

18 My book quiz

▸ p. 90

How well do you know your student's book? Test yourself! Give short answers.

1 The capital of Australia is …	Canberra
2 The name of the rock that is important to the Aboriginal culture is …	Uluru
3 Name three Australian animals.	Koala, kangaroo, emu
4 Your … tells others about your education and work experience.	CV
5 When you apply for a job, you must also send a letter of …	application
6 The time of learning and training for a job is called …	an apprenticeship
7 UK courts can give young trouble-makers an …	ASBO
8 In the US trouble-makers can choose to go to a … instead of prison.	boot camp
9 Which city has the biggest population: Mumbai, Johannesburg or Berlin?	Mumbai
10 Soweto is a famous township of which city?	Johannesburg
11 About how many people live in Berlin?	3.4 million
12 When was the Fall of the Berlin Wall?	November 1989

4819
4820

How well can you do these things?	Very well	OK	Practise!
LISTENING AND READING SKILLS: I can ...			
... read longer fictional and non-fictional texts without difficulty, e.g. *The caller* (SB pp. 62–64).	☐	☐	☐
... follow a class presentation (e.g. about Berlin).	☐	☐	☐
SPEAKING AND WRITING SKILLS: I can ...			
... structure, prepare and give a class presentation.	☐	☐	☐
... take part in a discussion, express my opinion, give reasons and examples, agree and disagree, e.g. about boot camps.	☐	☐	☐
... write an outline for a written discussion, with arguments and examples for and against a statement. I can sum up the main points with my personal opinion, e.g. on the use of mobiles at school.	☐	☐	☐
... write a formal letter of enquiry.	☐	☐	☐
MEDIATION SKILLS: I can ...			
... summarize and report a conversation or written text from German into English or from English into German, e.g. about volunteer work.	☐	☐	☐
... use my own words when I tell somebody about something. I do not translate the original conversation or written text.	☐	☐	☐
TOPICS: I have learned ...			
... about problems of big cities like Mumbai, Johannesburg and Berlin, e.g. pollution, crime, unemployment, overcrowding.	☐	☐	☐
... about the apartheid system in South Africa and what it meant for black citizens.	☐	☐	☐
... about teenage activities, interests and hobbies, e.g. mobile behaviour, relationships, volunteer work and community service.	☐	☐	☐
... about problems of teenagers who behave anti-socially, and about punishments for anti-social behaviour, e.g. ASBOs and boot camps.	☐	☐	☐
STUDY AND LANGUAGE SKILLS: I know ...			
... how to create visual materials (e.g. posters, overhead transparencies, maps, charts, timelines) and use them in presentations.	☐	☐	☐

HOW I COULD IMPROVE MY ENGLISH SKILLS: I could ...

(e.g. work through parts of Skills Check 2 again, find an English-speaking online friend, ...)

____

____

____

____

____

LISTENING

In this part of your workbook you will find exercises that will help you with your skills: listening, reading, writing, speaking, mediation.

1 Chat in the break (Listening for gist) ▸ WB (p. 71) 16

Listen to four short dialogues. What are the friends talking about? Match the number to the topic.

1	the school team
2	a project
3	weekend plans
4	a school trip

Tip 1

Look at the four topics. **Which words/ word fields** might you expect to hear? Listen for those words.
For example:
project > *research, subject, finish*
school trip > *bus/train, place, time*
weekend plans > *friends, party*
school team > *match, game, play*

2 The Olympic Games (Listening for gist) ▸ WB (p. 71) 17

Read statements A–E. Then listen to four students talking about the Olympic Games. Match the statements to the students. Write the correct letter in the box. There is one statement/letter that you do not need.

A I'm a sporty person, so I love the summer Olympics.
B I think the Olympic Games have become too political.
C The Games have become too spectacular and too expensive.
D I'm not into sport, so I don't really follow the Games on TV.
E We can all learn a lot from Olympic athletes.

5002 Student 1: E Student 2: A Student 3: D Student 4: C

Tip 2

Before you listen, concentrate[1] on the statements A–E.
Decide which are **positive** and which are **negative**. Mark **key words** and listen for them.
Notice how the speakers give their opinion. Is their **tone** of voice positive or negative?

3 Tricky numbers, times, letters (Listening for detail) ▸ WB (p. 71) 18

Listen and mark what you hear: one from each pair.

a)	245 / 254	14 / 40	98 / 89	60 / 16	
	02256691 / 02256651	1978 / 1987			
b)	2.30 / 2.13	12.30 / 1.30	4.30 / 3.30	9.15 / 9.50	
c)	A / E	E / I	A / R	G / J	J / G

5003

Tip 3

When you listen the first time, write down **names**, **places**, **dates**, **numbers**, **times** or **letters** exactly. When you listen a second time, check your notes and concentrate on the answers you still need.

4 At the station (Listening for detail) ▸ WB (p. 71) 19

You are going to hear three short train announcements. First read the statements below carefully. Then listen to the announcements and tick the correct box.

	True	False
1 The train to Edinburgh will leave from platform 6.	[x]	[ ]
2 The train will leave 13 minutes later.	[ ]	[x]
3 The 12.15 train to Bristol will not leave from platform 9 today.	[x]	[ ]
4 The Bristol train will now leave from platform 7E.	[ ]	[x]
5 The train from York will now arrive at platform 3 at 12.43.	[ ]	[x]

5004

Tip 4

Look exactly at the details in the questions, for example prepositions: ***from***, ***to***, ***at***. Then listen for them. For example, did you hear 'from' or 'to'?

[1] concentrate ['kɒnsntreɪt] *sich konzentrieren*

5 The London Eye (Listening for detail) ▸ *WB (p. 71)* 🎧 20

Listen to a guide telling tourists about the London Eye. Then choose the correct answer A, B or C.

1 The tourists' ride on the London Eye is booked[1] for …

A 2.30 pm. B 3.30 pm. C 4.30 pm.

2 How far can you see on a clear day?

A 40 miles. B 40 kilometres. C 14 kilometres.

3 When did work on the London Eye start?

A 1990. B 1991. C 1992.

4 How many passenger[2] capsules[3] are there?

A 23. B 25. C 32.

5105 5 The London Eye is now the … biggest wheel in the world.

A second B third C fourth

Tip 5

Often information is given **indirectly**, in different words.
For example:
When did work on the Eye start?
You hear only:
It took 7 years to build and it was opened in 1999. But you can work out the answer from this information.

6 BE and AE (BE and AE pronunciation) ▸ *WB (p. 71)* 🎧 21, 22, 23

a) *Listen to the words (🎧 21). Is the pronunciation BE or AE? Write AE (American English) or BE (British English) in the box. If you are not sure, listen again.*

1	BE	5	AE	9	BE
2	AE	6	AE	10	AE
3	BE	7	BE	11	AE
4	AE	8	AE	12	BE

5106

Tip 6

	BE	AE
grass, can't	[a:]	[æ]
knew, Tuesday	[ju:]	[u:]
not, got	[ɒ]	[ɑ]
first, world, more >	in AE you hear the 'r'	
little, city, writer >	in AE 't' in the middle of a word sounds like 'd'	

b) *Now look carefully at these sentences. Mark the sounds which are pronounced differently in AE. Then listen (🎧 22) and check that you have marked all the differences. You'll hear each sentence twice: first in BE, then in AE.*

1 It's so hot in here! Let's go to the park! I'll ask my sister if she wants to join us.

2 Let's have a drink first. How about a glass of mineral water? Or some coffee?

3 I forgot to tell you. We have a new student in our class. It's her birthday soon. She's invited us all to a party.

c) *You're in a tourist information office in London. Listen to what people are asking (🎧 23). Are they British or American? Write the number of each speaker under the UK or the US flag.*

Speakers 2, 5, 7

Speakers 1, 3, 4, 6, 8

[1] book [bʊk] *buchen* [2] passenger ['pæsɪndʒə] *Passagier, Fahrgast* [3] capsule ['kæpsju:l] *Kapsel*

7 At the youth hostel (Accents) ▸ WB (p. 71) 🎧 24

*You hear some young people talking about why tourists like to visit their countries. Do they come from the **UK**, the **USA** or **Australia**? Write the country under the photo.*

5207 1 UK 2 Australia 3 USA 4 Australia 5 USA 6 UK

8 In a café (Fast speech) ▸ WB (p. 71) 🎧 25, 26

a) *Listen to three teenagers talking about their problems (🎧 25). They are talking at a normal speed[1], but in everyday speech some words are shortened or missed out. Listen for the forms in **Tip 7** too. Who says what? Write the names in 1–4 below: **Todd**, **Will** or **Liz**.*

1 Liz and Todd are having problems with their parents.

2 Todd 's parents are not so strict with his younger brother.

3 Will doesn't know how to solve[3] his problem with his girlfriend.

4 Liz is having problems at school with her grades.

Tip 7

When people talk quickly, they may use words or phrases that are not grammatically correct. You hear the following forms especially[2] in AE. Maybe you've heard these forms in song lyrics too:

gonna > *going to*
wanna > *want to*
gotta > *have got to*
kinda > *kind of*
dunno > *don't know*

b) *Listen to the rest of the conversation (🎧 26). This time the friends are talking faster. Listen carefully for short forms as in a) above. Then tick true or false.*

	True	False
1 Liz doesn't want to give up her weekend job.	✔	
2 Liz thinks she'll talk to her Maths teacher and her Science teacher.		✔
3 Will's girlfriend is called Katie.		✔
4 Will doesn't always work on Friday evenings.	✔	
5 Will has a job at a pizza place.		✔
6 Will has a friend called Matt.	✔	
7 Will's girlfriend went to a movie with a boy called Stevie.		✔
8 Todd says Will has to trust[4] his girlfriend more.	✔	

[1] speed [spi:d] *Geschwindigkeit* [2] especially [ɪˈspeʃəli] *besonders* [3] solve [sɒlv] *lösen* [4] trust [trʌst] *vertrauen*

9 Talking about jobs (Listening skills) ▸ *WB (p. 71)* 27

a) *Listen to five young people talking about jobs. First, read the statements below and the list of names. Then listen to what they say. Choose the correct statement below for each person. Write A–E next to the names.*

A ‘I’ve found a job as a waitress in a café, but I won’t find out details until I call again later today.’

B ‘I had a big problem on my first day. The manager wasn’t very happy.’

C ‘I’ve applied for lots of jobs I got from the job centre. I’ve had one job offer so far.’

D ‘I enjoy my work now, but at first I wasn’t allowed to serve customers because I had to learn the job.’

E ‘I wanted to work with computers, but I’m learning to repair cars now. I like it.’

Dylan: C Sophie: A Gina: D Jamie: E Leo: B

b) *Now listen again, this time for details. Choose the correct answer and tick the box.*

1 Dylan is looking for …
[ ] a summer job. [ ] a job after school. [x] a Saturday job.

2 Dylan found some jobs at the job centre, and he has applied for …
[ ] four. [x] five. [ ] six.

3 Sophie already has some job experience …
[ ] in a hotel. [ ] in a café. [x] in a restaurant.

4 Sophie has to call again about the job at …
[ ] 1.30. [x] 2.30. [ ] 3.30.

5 Gina is from …
[x] Australia. [ ] the UK. [ ] the USA.

6 Gina works in a flower shop …
[ ] from nine to five. [x] from nine to six. [ ] after school.

7 Jamie has a …
[ ] part-time job. [ ] holiday job. [x] full-time job.

8 Jamie works in …
[ ] Glasgow. [x] Aberdeeen. [ ] a village near Aberdeen.

9 Leo has been working in a travel agency[1] …
[x] for a week. [ ] for a month. [ ] since he left school.

10 Leo sent the wrong flight tickets to Mrs White. She wanted to go to …
[ ] Johannesburg. [x] Hawaii. [ ] Alaska.

[1] travel agency [ˈeɪdʒənsiː] *Reisebüro*

READING

10 ESL in L.A. (1) (Skimming) ▸ WB (p. 72)

You would like to visit L. A. and maybe do an English course. You find this information on the internet. Who is the information for? Skim the text for a few seconds. Then tick A, B or C.

The information is for [A] American college students. [B] teachers of ESL. [C ✓] foreign students of English.

English as a second language (ESL) in L.A.

ESL programs	Our programs cover all areas of English as a second language. We offer **intensive programs** and exam preparation programs for college and university entrance.
Course levels	We offer courses for **beginners**, **intermediate** and **advanced** levels[1]. All levels have training in reading, listening, speaking and writing skills, vocabulary building, pronunciation and grammar. Courses in **American culture**, English for **business and commerce**, English for **science and technology** are offered at intermediate and advanced levels only.
Course hours	9 am – 12 am, 2 pm – 5 pm or 6 pm – 9 pm, Mon – Fri. There are no weekend courses.
Course groups	**Intensive programs**: groups of 6–8 students. All other course groups: 12–15 students.
Teaching staff	All our teachers are college and university trained professionals and are native speakers.
Location	Centrally located close to city attractions, shopping and eating within walking distance.
Accommodation[2]	Students may choose to stay with a selected **host family**[3] or at a **residence club** (single room with breakfast and dinner).

5410

Tip 8

Step 1: Look at the **form** of the text. Is it a newspaper article, a short story, an information brochure?
Step 2: Look at the **title**, **headings** and **pictures**.
Step 3: Look at the words in **bold** type.

11 ESL in L.A. (2) (Scanning) ▸ WB (p. 72)

*Now scan the text in exercise 10 above to find the answers to the questions below. The key words are in **bold**. Write short answers.*

1 What does **ESL** mean? *English as a second language*

2 How many **course levels** are offered? *3*

3 Do all courses teach **American culture**? *no*

4 Where is the school **located**? *centrally, close to attractions/shops*

5 Are there any courses at the **weekend**? *no*

6 How many students are there in the **intensive** programme groups? *6–8*

7 How many kinds of **accommodation** does the school help with? *2*

5411 8 Can students stay with a host family and have their own room? *yes*

Tip 9

Concentrate only on the **key words** in the questions when you scan. Read **around** a key word to find the answer. Remember, you may find a key word in one or more places in the text.

[1] advanced level [əd'vɑːnst 'levl] *fortgeschrittenes Niveau* [2] accommodation [əˌkɒmə'deɪʃn] *Unterkunft* [3] host family [həʊst] *Gastfamilie*

12 Getting into London (Marking key words, taking notes) ▸ *WB (p. 72)*

*a) You are flying to London, so you need information about different kinds of transport into London from Heathrow Airport. Choose and mark **key words** for the most important details.*

Getting into London from Heathrow

From Heathrow Airport you can take a train, the tube, a coach or a taxi into London.

1 If you want to go by train, the Heathrow Express takes you to Paddington Station in just 15–20 minutes. Trains run every 15 minutes. Cost: £ 16.50.
2 By tube the journey takes 45 minutes. Heathrow is on the Piccadilly line. There are three tube stations at the airport serving different terminals. The tube stops at famous places in the capital such as Hyde Park Corner, Piccadilly Circus and Covent Garden. Tube trains leave every five minutes. Cost: £4.50
3 You can take the National Express coach from the Central Bus Station (near Terminals 1, 2 and 3) to Victoria Coach Station in central London. The journey by coach takes 45–75 minutes. There are three to six buses an hour. Cost: £5.
4 By black taxi the journey takes 30–75 minutes. Cost for up to five passengers: £40–70.

(Prices: February 2010)

b) From your key words, write short notes about the different kinds of transport.

1 train: Heathrow Express to Paddington, 15-20 min., every 15 min., £16.50

2 tube: 45 min., Piccadilly line, three tube stations at the airport, every five min., £4.50

3 coach: National Express, from Central Bus Station to Victoria Coach Station, 45-75 min., three-six buses per hour, £5

4 taxi: 30-75 min., £40-70

13 Florida's Marine Park (Reading for detail) ▸ *WB (p. 72)*

Before you scan the text about Marine Park, read the statements on the next page. Mark key words in the statements, then look for the answers in the text and tick true, false or not given.

Tip 10

If there are no or not many words in **bold** in the text, choose your own **key words** from the questions. Look for them when you scan the text and read **around** them to find the answers.

Opening times
Marine Park is open to visitors every day from 9 am to 7 pm, and from 9 am to 9 pm in the summer months and at holiday times.

How to get here
If you are driving you will find us just 10 miles northwest of downtown Tampa. From Tampa International Airport it's just a 20-minute taxi ride. Our main entrance[1] and car park for 3,500 vehicles are on South Marine Drive. You can't miss us! Please visit our website for detailed directions.

Admission
1-day tickets: Adults $ 83.95 (plus tax[2]), children 3–10 years $ 69.95 (plus tax). Children two years and under go free. Senior citizens[3] pay less. Online tickets: For tickets bought online 7 days before your visit, there is a standard price of $69.95 (plus tax). You can print your ticket at home and there's no waiting at the park entrance.
Florida visitors: Please see our special online offers for 1-day and 3-day tickets.
5513 Florida residents[4]: Please see our special annual and vacation offers.

[1] entrance ['entrəns] *Eingang* [2] tax [tæks] *Steuer* [3] senior citizen ['siːniə 'sɪtɪzn] *Rentner/in* [4] resident [rezɪdənt] *Bewohner/in*

	True	False	Not given
1 The park is open all year round from 9 am to 9 pm.		✔	
2 Marine Park is northwest of Tampa.	✔		
3 It's a 30-minute drive from Tampa International Airport.		✔	
4 You enter Marine Park from South Marine Drive.	✔		
5 Adult tickets are cheaper online.	✔		
6 There is no US tax on tickets.		✔	
7 You can use online tickets for one year.			✔
8 There are special ticket offers for Florida residents.	✔		
9 You can buy Quick Queue tickets.			✔
10 Children under three years of age are free.	✔		

14 Marine Park visitor information (Reading for detail) ▸ WB (p. 72)

Read the visitor information sign carefully. It is not important to understand all the words when you read the first time. Complete the sentences below with words from the sign.

Marine Park Visitor Information

Welcome to Marine Park. Before visitors enter the park all bags will be examined by our security staff. It is not permitted to bring sharp or dangerous objects into the park, including pocket knives, cans and glass bottles. Please leave these objects in your vehicle.

Visitors are asked not to bring food and drinks into the park. Restaurants and stands selling snacks and soft drinks can be found in several park areas.

All indoor areas of the park are smoke-free. Outdoor smoking areas are clearly marked on your park map. If you wish to smoke, please do so in these areas only.

Information about animal feeding times can be found in the park map. Please do not try to feed the animals. It's bad for the animals and may be dangerous for you.

If you wish to bring along your pets, they can wait for you in our pets' area near the main entrance. We ask you to walk your dog regularly during your park visit and to bring along enough pet food. Your pets will be safe and well-looked after for just $12 a day.

For safety reasons, visitors are not allowed to take objects into the park which are *dangerous* ________. You can buy soft drinks and snacks in the park, so you are asked not to bring your own *food and drinks* ________. *Smoking* ________ is only allowed in clearly marked areas. Please follow the signs. Details of *animal feeding times* ________ can be found in the *park map* ________. There's also a service that looks after visitors' *pets* ________, so you can bring along your dog or cat too – for just $12 a day.

Tip 11

The words in the task are often different from the words in the text. But the meaning is the same.
Work out the meaning of **unknown words** from the **context**, for example: *examine, cans, vehicle.*

15 What does it mean? (Working out the meaning of words) ▸ WB (p. 71)

Look at the text in exercise 14 again. How did you work out the meaning of unknown words? Write the words in the lists with their German meaning. If a word fits into two lists, decide what helped you most.

examined • staff • permitted • sharp • vehicle • stand • regular • several • entrance • well-looked after

... from the context		... like a German word		... from a part of the word or the word family	
staff	Personal	sharp	scharf	examined	kontrolliert,
permitted	gestattet	vehicle	Vehikel,		überprüft,
several	mehrere,		Fahrzeug	entrance	Eingang
	einige	stand	Stand	well-looked	
		regular	regulär,	after	gut versorgen
			regelmäßig		

5715

16 Saving our planet (Reading skills) ▸ WB (pp. 71–72)

Read part of a text about the earth's problems. You don't have to understand all the words the first time you read.

Saving our planet

1 Climate change is thought by scientists to be a major problem. In less than a hundred years from now, the earth's average temperature could have risen by as much as five degrees. People living in cold countries may like the idea, but the temperature rise would put the earth and its peoples in danger, as a warmer climate would have disastrous effects on the future of man and nature.

2 A main cause is that humans produce 'greenhouse gases', for example, when burning oil, gas or wood for energy. Industries are a major cause of this. CO2 is released into the atmosphere. This leads to the 'greenhouse effect', as the sun's heat is trapped by too many greenhouse gases in the atmosphere, so the earth gets warmer. Deforestation is another cause, as forests and rainforests absorb carbon dioxide.

3 The effects of global warming could be catastrophic. The ice at the poles could melt, so sea levels would rise – maybe by up to two metres in the next 150 years, some experts believe. This would mean that cities like New York, London or Tokyo might slowly disappear under the sea. Millions of people could be permanently homeless. Some countries could become seriously overpopulated. There may be more natural disasters, like tsunamis and tornadoes. Tropical diseases would spread more quickly into non-tropical countries. The heat could dry up the food we grow. Food prices would rise and millions could become hungry. There might not be enough drinking water, so wars might start. Some animals and plants might die out because they could not survive in saltwater.

4 In order to slow down climate change, we must reduce global warming, for example, by using less energy in our daily lives. We should stop burning oil and gas, which produce carbon dioxide and are non-renewable. We should use more renewable energy like solar or wind power. We should save electricity and water, and produce less waste by recycling. We could buy recyclable and energy-efficient products (light bulbs, fridges, computers, etc.). We could plant more trees. We must stop cutting down rainforests. All this and much more ...

a) Choose a suitable heading for each paragraph. Write A–D in the boxes.

Paragraph 1 [B] Paragraph 2 [D] Paragraph 3 [C] Paragraph 4 [A]

A Solutions[1] B Problems C Consequences D Reasons

b) Look at the text again. How can you work out the meaning of the unknown words? Write the following words in lists 1–3 with their German meaning. Some words fit into two lists. Decide what helped you most.

climate • scientist • nature • cause • lead • greenhouse effect • release • heat • trapped • deforestation • poles • melt • expert • permanent • disaster • tropical • dry up • reduce • renewable • power • recyclable • energy-efficient

1 I can understand these words from the **context**: lead (führen), heat (Hitze), release (abgeben), trapped (gefangen), melt (schmelzen), dry up (austrocknen)

2 These words are like **German** words: climate, nature, poles, expert, permanent, disaster, tropical, reduce, power, energy-efficient

3 I know **part** of these words or a word from the **word family**: scientist (Wissenschaftler/in), cause (Grund), greenhouse effect (Treibhauseffekt), deforestation (Abholzung), renewable (erneuerbar), recyclable (recycelbar)

c) Read the statements below carefully and tick the correct box.

	True	False	Not in the text
1 At the end of this century the earth's temperature could be a few degrees warmer.	✔		
2 Households produce about a third of greenhouse gases.			✔
3 CO2 is a 'greenhouse gas'.	✔		
4 Natural gas is a renewable source of energy.		✔	
5 A lot of the waste we produce finds its way into the seas.			✔
6 Recyclable products help to reduce waste.	✔		
7 Rainforests are burned down so that cattle farmers can produce more meat for export.			✔
8 CO2 cannot be absorbed.		✔	

d) Now complete these sentences with information from the text.

1 Climate change is thought to be a major problem because a warmer climate could put the earth in danger./change the future of man and nature.

2 We all produce 'greenhouse gases' by burning oil, gas or wood for energy.

3 The earth gets warmer because the sun's heat is trapped by greenhouse gases in the atmosphere.

4 If the ice at the poles melted, sea levels would rise. As a result, cities like New York, London or Tokyo might slowly disappear under the sea.

5 People wouldn't have enough to eat because the heat could dry up the food that we grow.

[1] solution [sə'luːʃn] *Lösung*

WRITING

17 Collecting ideas (Brainstorming) ▸ WB (pp. 72–74)

a) Choose three topics from A–F below. Brainstorm ideas that you could use, for example in an e-mail to a friend. Make a list or a mindmap for each of your three topics in your exercise book.

A My free time
B A great holiday
C My ideal job
D Work experience
E My best birthday
F Raising money for charities

A great holiday
2 making new friends
disco
pool
1 sightseeing
historic buildings
~~hotel~~ ...

Tip 12
Remember to cross out ideas you won't use and number the useful ideas.

b) Use your notes from a) to write an e-mail to an American friend about one of your topics. Write 80–100 words in your exercise book.

Hi ...!
Thanks for the mail and the cool photos of your holiday trip to Miami. You wanted to know about my holiday in ... It was great too, so I'll tell you about it.
Well, ...
...

18 Giving information (The 5 Ws) ▸ WB (pp. 73–74)

a) Whatever kind of text you write, your reader needs basic facts. Who or what is the text about? What happens or takes place? When, where and why does it happen or take place? The text below reports a street accident. In what order does it answer the 5 Ws?

Tip 13
The **5 Ws** are important both in reading and writing.
In a good story or report, you find answers to most of the *5 Ws* in the first two or three sentences. *Why...?* and *How...?* sometimes come later but are not always necessary.
The order of the information is not important and is usually different from text to text.

Teenager hit by cyclist[1]
At 10.30 last night a 15-year-old girl was hurt by a cyclist as she was crossing Radfield Road on her way home after visiting a friend. The cyclist, who admitted[2] that he was riding too fast on the empty road, ran into the girl, who was wearing dark clothes. The cyclist said, 'She came from nowhere. I just didn't see her.' The cyclist called an ambulance and the girl was treated[3] for a broken finger and shock.

1 When? at 10.30 last night
2 Who? a 15-year-old girl
3 What? was hurt by a cyclist
4 Where? Radfield Road
5918
5 Why? the cyclist was riding too fast, he didn't see the girl

b) Now write a short text about your last school trip. Give information about the 5 Ws in the first few sentences, as in the text in a). **Who** *went (students, teachers),* **where** *you went,* **when** *you went,* **how** *you got there,* **what** *you did there. Write 60–80 words in your exercise book.*

Last year our class went on a trip to ... with ... / Our last class trip took place in ... this year ...

[1] cyclist ['saɪklɪst] *Radfahrer/in* [2] admit [əd'mɪt] *zugeben* [3] treat [triːt] *behandeln*

19 Making changes ▸ *WB (pp. 73–74)*

Tip 14

You can:
- change active to passive or passive to active.
- add a subordinate clause.
- change direct to indirect speech.
- make one sentence out of two using a linking word.
- change the linking word (e.g. *so* > *because*, *but* > *although*).

a) *Here are some tips that will help you when you want to write a text. Read* **Tip 14** *and study the following examples carefully.*

1 After three days the police caught the escaped thief. They had been told where they could find him.
Change active to passive and passive to active.
The escaped thief was caught after a few days. Someone had told the police where to find him.

2 It was a cold day in winter when Leila packed her bags and left home to start a new life in Pakistan. She had never met the man who was going to be her husband.
Add a relative clause – *where* ..., and make one sentence out of two.
On a cold winter day Leila left home for Pakistan, where she would start a new life with a husband she had never met.

3 'I'll never be able to wear jeans and tops again,' Leila thought sadly.
Change direct to indirect speech. Use group words not details – *western clothes for jeans and tops.*
Leila was sad that she would never be able to wear western clothes again.

4 After breakfast, Rob and Pete started their bike tour. The sun was shining. There were only a few white clouds in the sky.
Make one sentence out of two with a linking word, here: *When* ... Leave out details of weather description.
When Rob and Pete started their cycle tour in the morning, the weather was very good.

5 Tom always needs money, so he does a newspaper round before school and he sometimes works in his cousin's café on Wilmore Street. He washes cars and does garden work for the neighbours too.
Change the linking word – *so* > *because*. Leave out unnecessary details of jobs.
Because Tom always needs money, he does lots of jobs before and after school.

b) *Now write the following sentences differently and shorten them where possible. Make one sentence. Remember to use what you have learned in a) above.*

1 It was really cold in the house, so Polly made a big pot of hot tea for everybody.

Polly made some hot tea because it was cold in the house.

2 US border police send back hundreds of illegal Mexican immigrants every week. Pedro was one of them.

Pedro was one of the hundreds of illegal Mexican immigrants who are sent back at the border every week.

3 Jerry arrived late at the airport because of a traffic jam on the motorway. He found that his plane to Vancouver had already left.

When Jerry finally arrived at the airport, his plane to Vancouver had left.

4 'There's so much to prepare before the visitors arrive – the flat to clean, shopping to do, food to cook,' thought Emily nervously.

Emily was nervous because there was so much to do before the visitors arrived.

20 Writing a formal letter

SF (p. 137)

a) *Complete the text with words and phrases that are correct for formal letters. If you need help, look in your student's book (p. 137).*

You put your own address at the top on the right, but you don't write your name. Under your address you write the date. The address of the person you are writing to is written on the left.

You begin a formal letter with 'Dear Sir or Madam' when you don't know the name of the person you are writing to. Remember that the first word of the first paragraph starts with a capital letter – which is different from German. You shouldn't use short forms in formal letters. Write 'I am' and 'I would' instead of 'I'm' and 'I'd.

You finish a formal letter with 'Yours faithfully' if you don't know the name of the person you are writing to. If you know the name, you start with 'Dear Mr/Mrs/Ms ...' and you finish with 'Yours sincerely'.

b) *Lisa Schneider from Munich writes a letter of application for a job as assistant receptionist[1] at a hotel in London for six weeks in summer. What belongs where in a formal letter? Choose the correct parts from the list on the right and write the number in the correct place in the letter below.*

8

4

9

5

7

6

2

Lisa Schneider
Lisa Schneider

1 Best wishes
2 Yours faithfully
3 Dear Mrs Wilson,
4 2nd May 2010
5 Dear Sir or Madam
6 I look forward to hearing from you.
7 I am writing to apply for the job of assistant receptionist as advertised on your website ...
8 Webergasse 8
81735 Munich
9 The Manager
Lancaster Hall Hotel
28 Lancaster Road
London W8 IJ

6120

Tip 15

British addresses:
Note that the house number comes **before** the name of the road or street, not after it.
Note also that in the UK the postcode comes **after** the town or city, not before it.

c) *If you wanted this job, how would you write your letter of application? Write the main text of your letter in your exercise book. Write about the following:*

- your age, personal details
- how long you have been learning English and how good your English is
- what kind of person you are, work experience, your hobbies and interests
- why you would like the job and why you think you could do it well.

[1] receptionist [rɪˈsepʃənɪst] *Rezeptionist/in*

21 Writing a CV ▸ SF (p. 136)

Lisa has to send her CV with the application. Here is the necessary information about her:

Her telephone number is 0049 89 612 37 97. Her mobile number is 0173 835 2380.
Her e-mail is: lschneider@arl.com
She was born in Munich on 23rd November 1995.

Lisa is a friendly, hard-working student who likes speaking English and enjoys meeting people. She is good at organizing and likes working in a team. She is punctual and reliable.
She has already worked as a waitress for six weeks in a hotel in Stockholm, Sweden, where she spoke English and German to hotel guests. Last year in the Easter holidays she also worked at the information desk in a shopping mall in Munich.
In her free time she likes reading and writing to online friends in the UK and the USA. She enjoys cooking, swimming and playing football.
Lisa was at a primary school in Augsburg from 2001 to 2005. She has been at a secondary school in Munich since 2005. She is taking her school-leaving exams (similar to GCSEs) this year. She has a good level of everyday English (6 years) and French (4 years). She also has good computer skills and a moped licence.

a) *In what order should Lisa present this information at the top of her CV? Write the numbers 1–4 after the headings.*

Postal address	2	E-mail address	4
Name	1	Mobile number	3

b) *What could Lisa write in her short personal statement?*

I am a friendly, hard-working and punctual person who enjoys meeting people and speaking English. I am also a good organizer and a reliable team worker.

Tip 16

Date and place of birth are not always given in English CVs, but it is useful for employers[1] to know your **age** and your **native language**[2] if you are applying for a job abroad.
The personal statement should not be longer than three short sentences. Use only long verb forms.

c) *In which order should she give details about the following? Write 1–6.*

Work experience	4	Hobbies and interests	5	Education	1
Qualifications	2	Reference(s)	6	Other skills	3

d) *Now use information from a) (information about Lisa) to write the CV sections in c), but leave out 'Reference(s)'. Remember to write in note form, not in full sentences.*

Education: 2001 – 2005 primary school in Augsburg, since 2005 secondary school in Munich

Qualifications: secondary school-leaving exams (similar to GCSEs) this year
Languages: English (6 years), French (4 years)

Other skills: good computer skills, moped licence

Work experience: waitress in a hotel in Stockholm (six weeks),
worked at information desk in a Munich shopping mall

Hobbies and interests: reading, writing to online friends in UK and USA, cooking, swimming, playing football

6221

e) *Write the CV on the computer using the correct format.*

[1] employer [ɪm'plɔɪə] *Arbeitgeber/in* [2] native language *Muttersprache*

22 Asking for information (Question forms) 28

When you ask for information, it is important to form questions correctly and quickly. How do the teenagers ask the questions below? Write in your exercise book. Then listen to your CD and check your answers.

1 Dana is at JFK airport in New York. She wants a bus to the town centre. She asks someone politely …
- *if they know where the buses leave from.*
- where the buses stop in the town centre.
- how long the bus ride takes.
- how much bus tickets cost.
- where you buy the bus tickets.

2 Patrick is having an interview for a holiday job at a garage. He asks the boss …
- *what he would have to do exactly.*
- what time the garage opens.
- if he would have to work on Saturdays.
- how many hours he would have to work a week.
- when he could start.

6322

23 Describing a picture (Brainstorming vocabulary) ▸ WB (pp. 72–73) 29

When you describe a picture you usually have to …

- say generally where it is, e.g. a scene in winter, a city street.
- what the background looks like, what is happening there.
- talk about the people (How many are there? Where are they?) and say what they are doing and what they are wearing.
- say how the people are probably feeling and what they are thinking.
- use adjectives to talk about the atmosphere of the picture.

a) *Look at the picture below and brainstorm your ideas for vocabulary. In your exercise book, write down words to describe the scene. If you don't know the words you need, use your dictionary.*

Tip 17

Useful phrases for talking about pictures:
The picture shows a scene in summer/at a beach/in a big city/in a hot country …
It looks as if people are having fun …
The woman/man on the right is laughing/chatting …
Maybe she/he is thinking that …
She might be …
The people look/seem to be happy/excited …

Tip 18

Answering questions
Express[1] your opinion and give reasons and arguments for it.
Here are some ideas:
I can't ski so I think summer holidays are better.
In my opinion, skiing holidays are too expensive.
I like holidays where I can …
I like swimming and I'd like to learn to snowboard too because …
Sport plays an important role in my free time. I … every week.

b) *Be prepared to answer general questions that have to do with the picture indirectly. Listen to the five questions on your CD (29). Answer each question with at least two complete sentences. You can make notes in your exercise book first. Then practise your answers, first from your notes, then without your notes. Concentrate on speaking clearly, but not too quickly.*

[1] express [ɪk'spres] *äußern, ausdrücken*

24 Comparing pictures ▸ WB (p. 72) 30

When you compare two pictures, you are expected to talk about differences and compare advantages and disadvantages.

a) *Think of words and phrases to talk about these pictures. Make lists.*

A

B

A In a town	B In the country
lots of people, cars, shops, noise,	few people, animals, forests, fields,
big buildings, dirty streets, dirty air,	paths, walking, hiking, hill-climbing,
loud, exciting, interesting, unfriendly people,	little traffic, fresh air, calm, quiet,
problems, traffic, accidents, police, ambulances,	healthy, farms, no theatres, no cinemas,
offices, theatres, good public transport,	boring, not many jobs, no schools,
shopping centres	have to travel, no public transport

b) *Use your notes in a) to discuss the two pictures.*

c) *You often have to discuss pictures or a given topic with your exam partner. Your dialogue should be realistic, so ask suitable questions. Here are some questions that you could ask about the topic of this exercise. Ask these questions in English, then check them on your CD (30).*

1 Wohnst du in der Stadt oder auf dem Land?

2 Würdest du lieber irgendwo anders wohnen?

3 Wie kommst du in die Schule?

4 Wo wohnen deine Freunde?

5 Welche Vorteile hat man auf dem Land?

6 Welche Vorteile hat man in der Stadt?

7 Hast du irgendwelche Großstädte im Ausland besucht?

8 Welche Großstadt hat dir am besten gefallen?

9 Wenn du nicht in Deutschland wohntest, wo würdest du wohnen wollen?

d) **Extra** *Ask your partner the questions 2–9 in c) in English.*

Tip 19

General advice
- You don't have to speak quickly, but you must speak clearly.
- Don't answer questions with *Yes* or *No* only.
- If you repeat an idea or opinion, say it differently.
- Say what you want, even if you think the examiner may not agree.

Tip 20

If you don't understand what the examiner/interviewer says, it's good to know some useful, polite **phrases** by heart.
Could you repeat that, please?
Could you explain that again/once more, please?
Sorry, I don't quite follow you.
Do you mean that I have to …?
Sorry, what exactly do I have to do?
Sorry, but I didn't quite understand/catch what you said.

Tip 21

Useful partner questions
When you have to talk to your exam partner, exchange information, give opinions, express feelings. You could start like this:
In my opinion, …
I have read that …
What do you think about …?
Don't you think that …?
Do you agree that …?
Isn't it better to … than to …?
What's your opinion about …?

MEDIATION

25 London travel (Mediating a written text) ▸ WB (p. 76)

a) *You are going to visit London with your family and you want to tell them the best way to travel around the city. You find this information. Mark the main facts first. Then make notes below in German.*

Tip 22

Mark the **main facts** and summarize them. Leave out unnecessary details. Don't translate.

London Travelcards for international visitors

If you are planning to travel in and around London, it's best to buy a Travelcard. You will save money and you will have complete freedom of travel on the Tube, buses, trams, Docklands Light Railway (DLR) and most local trains across the whole of London. You can even get riverboat tickets one third cheaper.

There are many different kinds of Travelcards. You have to choose whatever is best for you. You can buy a Travelcard for just one day, three days, seven days or even longer. London is divided into 6 travel zones and Travelcards cover different zones. Zones 1 and 2 cover Central London and most of the famous London sights. Zone 6 takes you to outer areas of the city, e.g. Heathrow Airport. You must decide which zones you want to visit.

You must also know at what time you want to start your journey. If you plan to travel before 9.30 am (Mon–Fri), you will need a Peak Travelcard. If you travel after 9.30 am, you can buy an Off-Peak Travelcard, which is a little cheaper. For example, an Off-Peak One-day Travelcard for Zones 1 and 2 costs £5.60 for an adult (16 and over). By comparison, the Peak One-day Travelcard costs £7.20. There are special reduced prices for children (5–15). Children under 5 go free. You can buy your Travelcard online, or all over the city at Tube stations and travel information centres.

(Prices: February 2010)

Travelcard – die günstigste Methode, London zu sehen; freie Fahrt in allen öffentlichen Verkehrsmitteln, Ermäßigung auf Bootsfahrkarten; London hat 6 Fahrzonen (Zonen 1 u. 2: Zentrum); wochentags billiger nach 9.30 am (Off-Peak); vor 9.30 am (Peak); erhältlich für 1 Tag, 3 Tage, 7 Tage oder länger; Preisbeispiel: Erwachsene – 1 Tag Off-Peak £5.60, Peak £7.20.

Tip 23

When you mediate written information, the order is not important. Before you start, find the main points. Sometimes it's easier to mark key words and note information under headings, here: **advantages, travel zones, journey times, prices.**

b) *You tell your parents what you have found out, but they still have a few questions. Give short answers in German.*

1 Wo kann man die Travelcard kaufen? Online, in Tube-Stationen, in Reisezentren

2 Kann man mit der Travelcard vom Flughafen in die Stadt fahren? ja

3 Du bist 16 und Schüler/in. Musst du schon den vollen Preis bezahlen? ja

4 Müssen wir für Tommy zahlen? Er ist ja erst vier. nein

26 What did he say? (Mediating what you hear) ▸ WB (p. 76) 31

Explain what you hear to your American exchange student. Listen to the radio programme and make a few notes while you are listening. Use your own words and tell him the main things in a few sentences.

He's talking about the 'Night Flyers'. They are coming to Germany on a concert tour at the end of March. Their first concert will be in Hamburg on 23rd March. The other concerts are in Berlin, Dresden and Stuttgart. The last concert is in Munich. You can buy tickets from tomorrow. After Germany they're going to Austria, Switzerland and Italy, and then to London for their last concert.

27 Explaining signs (Using modal auxiliaries)

You are in town with your dog, your bike and your British cousin. How can you explain these German signs to her? Tick the correct answers.

Tip 24

Be careful!
you can't ...
du kannst/darfst nicht ...
you have to ...
du musst ...
you don't have to .../you needn't ...
du musst/brauchst nicht ...
you must ...
du musst ...
you mustn't ...
du darfst nicht ...

1 

WIR MÜSSEN DRAUSSEN BLEIBEN

- [x] We can't take the dog in there.
- [ ] Dogs are allowed inside.
- [x] Dogs have to stay outside.

2 PARKEN VERBOTEN
Bitte keine Fahrräder abstellen!

- [x] You can't leave your bike here.
- [x] You mustn't leave your bike here.
- [x] You aren't allowed to leave your bike here.

3 Ganztägig geöffnet
Tischreservierung nicht erforderlich

- [x] You needn't book a table.
- [ ] You should book a table.
- [x] You don't have to book a table.

4 Konzertkarten
Bitte hier anstellen.

- [x] You can buy concert tickets here.
- [x] You have to stand in line.

5 Betreten des Turms
AUF EIGENE GEFAHR

- [ ] You mustn't go up the tower.
- [x] You can go up the tower but at your own risk[1].
- [x] You shouldn't really go up the tower.

6 RUHEZONE! MOBILTELEFONE
BITTE AUSSCHALTEN!

- [x] You have to be quiet.
- [x] You aren't allowed to use your mobile.
- [ ] You needn't turn off your mobile.

7 STADTBIBLIOTHEK
Haupteingang wegen Renovierungsarbeiten geschlossen. Bitte Nebeneingang links um die Ecke benutzen.

- [x] We can't use the main entrance[2].
- [x] We have to use the side entrance.

6627

[1] risk [rɪsk] *Risiko* [2] main entrance ['meɪn ˌentrəns] *Haupteingang*

28 Christmas on the beach (Simple present and present progressive) ▸ GF (p. 145)

Complete the text with the correct form: simple present (e.g. she goes) or present progressive (e.g. she is going).

This year Mike from Bristol is spending (spend) Christmas in Sydney with his Australian girlfriend Maggie. Like hundreds of other young people, they are celebrating (celebrate[1]) on Bondi Beach. At the moment they are swimming (swim) in the sea. Maggie knows (know) about the dangers of the ozone hole and how quickly the sun burns (burn) your skin, so she doesn't lie (not lie[2]) in the sun on the beach. And she never goes (go) to the beach at midday when it gets (get) really hot. But lots of young Britons, like Mike, don't seem (not seem) to worry about that.

6728

Tip 25

The **simple present** is important in everyday communication: writing/talking about yourself and others, what you often do, like, think.
You also need it for writing:
- summaries of stories, film and book reviews
- descriptions of characters in fictional texts
- comments on opinions/ideas
- your personal statement on your CV.

Tip 26

Use the **present progressive** for actions and situations that are going on at the time.
Remember, some verbs are not used in the progressive form:
believe, belong, know, like, need, own, seem.

29 He didn't understand (Simple past or past progressive) ▸ GF (p. 146)

Complete the text with verbs in the simple past or past progressive. There are some negative and some question forms.

Lisa wanted (want) to improve her English, so last year she applied for a job as au pair in the USA. She didn't know (not know) much about her American host family[3], but when she arrived (arrive) in Atlanta, all five members of her host family were waiting (wait) at the airport to meet her. While Lisa was chatting (chat) to Mrs Jackson about the flight, Mr Jackson picked (pick) up her large bag, but Lisa said (say) loudly, 'Oh, no, Mr Jackson. You mustn't carry my bag.' So Mr Jackson suddenly put (put) the bag down again. He looked (look) puzzled because he didn't understand (not understand). Why did Lisa want (Lisa/want) to carry the heavy[4] bag herself? Did she have (she/have) something important in her bag, or something that might break? Mr Jackson didn't say (not say) anything. When they were walking (walk) out of the airport, Lisa thought (think), 'Why did he put (he/put) my bag down? Is it too heavy for him? What's the problem?'
Do you know?

Tip 27

Use the **simple past** for completed actions in the past, often with signal words - *yesterday, last year* etc. Use it in stories or reports, or to talk about *when* something happened.
Make questions and negtives with *'did'*.
Use the **past progressive** for actions that were not completed at a time in the past.

[1] celebrate ['selɪbreɪt] *feiern* [2] lie [laɪ] *liegen* [3] host family [həʊst] *Gastfamilie* [4] heavy ['hevɪ] *schwer*

30 Saying it differently (Changing sentence structure)

You often have to say something differently without changing the meaning. Use the word in brackets to express the meaning in a different way.

Tip 28

It is important to say something differently when you:
- write a summary.
- mediate what someone says.
- answer questions about a text.
- take notes from a written text.

1 The phone rang while Mel was watching her favourite soap. (during)
The phone rang during Mel's favourite soap.

2 It was her boyfriend. The last time she had seen him was three days ago. (for)

She hadn't seen him for three days.

3 'Come to see the new film at the Gloria with me,' he said. (wanted)

He wanted her to come to see the new film at the Gloria with him.

4 There was a long queue at the cinema, so they had to wait. (because)

They had to wait because there was a long queue at the cinema.

5 The film wasn't as bad as the last one they had seen. (better)

The film was better than the last one they had seen.

31 The flying doctors of Australia (RFDS) (Using linking words) ▸ WB (p. 73)

Join two sentences with the linking word in brackets. Change the order of the sentences only where necessary.

1 About 10% of Australians live far away from towns and cities.
They can't get medical help easily. (so)

About 10% of Australians live far away from towns and cities, so they can't get medical help easily.

2 Before the RFDS started, many people died. Doctors could not reach them. (because)

Before the RFDS started, many people died because doctors could not reach them.

3 The Service is very well organized. It can reach people in over 80% of the country. (so)

The Service is very well organized, so it can reach people in over 80% of the country.

4 The RFDS has set up more than 20 bases all over the country. Doctors can reach people quickly. (so that)

The RFDS has set up more than 20 bases all over the country, so that doctors can reach people quickly.

5 It is not easy to pass the tests and interviews. Lots of young people apply to the RFDS. (although)

Although it is not easy to pass the tests and interviews, lots of young people apply to the RFDS.

6 The RFDS was started in about 1930. The RFDS is a 24-hour service. (which)

6831

The RFDS, which is a 24-hour service, was started in about 1930.

32 Explaining words (Paraphrasing) ▸ WB (p. 72)

If you don't know the English word for what you want to say, you can paraphrase it. Paraphrasing is useful in mediation. You can use:

It's someone who …/It's something (that) …/
It's a/the place where …

I'd like to be a – erm,
in German it's 'Regisseur'.
It's someone who knows a lot
about film-making and
directs films.

You are talking to your American exchange student about jobs and workplaces. Explain these words in English:

1 Tontechniker/in: It's someone who works in a recording studio and checks sound equipment at live concerts.

2 Mikrofon: It's something that makes your voice louder when you talk or sing to an audience.

3 Landschafts-gärtner/in: It's someone who designs and plans gardens and parks.

4 Schubkarre: It's something a builder or a gardener uses to push/move things in.

5 Rezeption: It is the place in a hotel where you can get information.

6932 6 Kasse: It's a place where you pay for things you have bought at a shop.

33 Making texts more interesting (Using adjectives)

a) *Choose three adjectives from the box that you could use in 1–4 below. Some adjectives fit into more than one list. Then add at least three more suitable adjectives to each list.*

boring · busy · clean · excited · exciting · healthy · interesting · noisy · polite · quiet · relaxing · serious

1 a job: boring, exciting, interesting, difficult, dangerous, useful

2 a town/city: busy, exciting, noisy, dangerous, old, modern

3 the countryside[1]: clean, healthy, quiet, beautiful, calm, lonely

4 a job candidate[2]: excited, polite, serious, careful, nervous, interested

b) *Write one or two sentences each about 1–4 in a). Use as many adjectives as you can from each list.*

1 I would like to have a job that's interesting and useful, not too difficult, and not boring. I don't want a dangerous job.

2 Berlin is a busy and exciting city with lots of history. It is the mix of old and modern buildings that makes it so interesting. Like all cities it is busy and noisy in some parts.

3 We live in a town but my parents love the countryside because it is quiet and beautiful. The air is clean and healthy too.

4 I hope I'll be a good job candidate one day. I'll try to be polite and serious at interviews. It's also important to be interested, but not too nervous.

[1] countryside ['kʌntrisaɪd] auf dem Land [2] candidate ['kændɪdət] *Kandidat/in, Bewerber/in*

34 About Simon (Word order in subordinate clauses) ▸ WB (p. 74)

Put the words in the boxes in the correct order to make subordinate clauses.

1 Since | school | Simon | left |, he has worked as a shop assistant.

Since Simon left school, he ...

2 Simon likes his work because | a lot of new things | learn | can | he |.

... he can learn a lot of new things.

3 Simon plays football for the local team, so | has to | he | train | twice a week |.

... he has to train twice a week.

4 If | well | he | works |, the manager lets him go home earlier.

If he works well, ...

5 That's usually on the days when | has to | he | football training | go to |.

... he has to go to football training.

6 The manager lets him go early because | of the local team | he | is | a big supporter |.

... he is a big supporter of the local team.

Tip 29

Word order in English is different from German. It is always **Subject-Verb-Object**. Compare:
*Since Simon **left** school, he has ...*
*Seitdem S. die Schule **verließ**, hat er ...*

35 A trip to New York (Correcting your text) ▸ WB (p. 74)

Here is Esma's e-mail to her online friend in Washington. Correct the mistakes.

Tip 30

Last but not least:
Always remember to read your texts carefully as soon as you finish them. Checking for mistakes is a very important part of any written exercise. Good luck!

Hi Kelly!
Here we are in New York! It's so cool here. I really enjoyed ~~planing~~ our sightseeing tour ~~befor~~ we came and we've done ~~the most~~ of the things on my list. We've been in New York ~~since~~ two days. The ~~whether~~ was great yesterday, so we ~~have gone~~ up the Empire State Building. I ~~made~~ some cool photos and I ~~heared~~ so ~~many~~ ~~over~~ the building. It was very ~~intresting~~. I have to talk English because my parents ~~want that I~~ ask a lot of questions about where ~~we must go~~ and what ~~we could do~~. ~~American~~ are very friendly and helpful. They always ~~say~~ me what I want to know. Maybe I could ~~travell~~ down to Washington ~~with the~~ train to see you for a day or two. Would that be OK? ~~I'm calling~~ you this evening. ~~Than~~ you can tell me what you ~~mean~~. If I ~~would come~~ to visit you, I'm sure we ~~had~~ lots of fun!
Esma

Correct

planning, before, most, for, weather, went, took, heard, much, about, interesting, want me to,

to go, to do, Americans, tell, travel, by, I'll call, Then, think, came, would have

7035

LISTENING SKILLS ▸ *pp. 127–129*

SF REVISION Listening for detail

Was muss ich allgemein beim *Listening* beachten?

Vor dem Hören:

- Lies dir die Fragen durch. So weißt du, worauf du beim Hören achten musst.
- Nutze Überschriften oder Bilder, um zu erahnen, um was es geht.
- Bereite dich darauf vor, Notizen zu machen. Leg z. B. eine Tabelle oder Liste an.

Beim Hören:

- Achte auf Geräusche, unterschiedliche Stimmen und wie Leute sprechen.
- Mach nur kurze Notizen, z. B. Symbole oder Stichworte, keine ganzen Sätze.
- Lass dich nicht verunsichern, wenn du mal einen Satz nicht verstehst.

Nach dem Hören:

- Vervollständige deine Notizen sofort.
- Achte beim zweiten Hören auf das, was du zuerst nicht gut verstanden hast.

Wie kann ich Einzelheiten (details) heraushören?

1. Mach dir bewusst, welche Einzelheiten du heraushören sollst bzw. willst. Lass dich von anderen Einzelheiten nicht ablenken.
2. Manche Signalwörter machen es dir leichter, den Hörtext zu verstehen:
   Aufzählung: **and**, **another**, **too**
   Gegensatz: **although**, **but**
   Grund, Folge: **because**, **so**, **so that**
   Vergleich: **larger/older/... than**, **more**, **most**
   Reihenfolge: **before**, **after**, **then**, **next**, **later**, **when**, **at last**, **at the same time**
3. Unterteile Telefonnummern beim Aufschreiben : **0171 572 45 89**.

SF REVISION Interactive listening

Beim Hören von Telefonansagen fehlt dir der Blickkontakt. Aber wenn du dich gut vorbereitest, kann dir nichts passieren.

Vor dem Hören:

- Überlege dir vorher, welche Informationen du suchst und auf welche Schlüsselwörter du dafür achten solltest. Schreibe sie auf.
- Geh zum Telefonieren möglichst an einen ruhigen Ort.

Beim Hören:

- Bleib ruhig! Du kannst eine Telefonansage mehrmals hören.
- Achte besonders darauf, ob du für deine Information eine Zahl drücken musst. Zahlen sagen dir, wie du die Ansage fortsetzen kannst. Oft werden sie auch wiederholt.
- Höre besonders genau zu, wenn deine Schlüsselworter genannt werden und mach dir Notizen zu ihnen.

Nach dem Hören:

- Geh das Gehörte noch mal in Gedanken durch. Hast du alles richtig verstanden und hast du alle Informationen? Wenn du nicht sicher bist, ruf einfach noch mal an. Es läuft ein Band und du störst niemanden.

REVISION READING COURSE – Zusammenfassung ▸ *pp. 130–131*

Working out the meaning of words

Das Nachschlagen unbekannter Wörter im Wörterbuch kostet Zeit und nimmt auf Dauer den Spaß am Lesen. Oft geht es auch ohne Wörterbuch!

Was hilft mir, unbekannte Wörter zu verstehen?

1. Bilder zeigen oft die Dinge, die du im Text nicht verstehst. Schau sie dir deshalb vor dem Lesen genau an.
2. Oft hilft dir der Textzusammenhang, z. B. **When we *reached* the station, Judy went to the ticket machine to buy our tickets.**
3. Zu manchen englischen Wörtern fallen dir vielleicht deutsche, französische oder lateinische Wörter ein, die ähnlich geschrieben oder ausgesprochen werden, z. B. **excellent**, **millionaire**, **nation**, **reality**.
4. Manchmal stecken in unbekannten Wörtern bekannte Teile, z. B. **friendliness**, **helpless**, **understandable**, **gardener**, **tea bag**.

Skimming and Scanning

Skimming: Lesen, um sich einen Überblick zu verschaffen

Beim **Skimming** überfliegst du einen Text schnell, um dir einen ersten Eindruck zu verschaffen, worum es geht. Das hilft dir herauszufinden, ob ein Text, den du im Internet oder einem Buch gefunden hast, überhaupt die Informationen enthält, nach denen du (z. B. für ein Referat) suchst. Achte dabei auf

- die **Überschrift**,
- die **Zwischenüberschriften** und **hervorgehobene** Wörter oder Sätze,
- die **Bilder** und **Bildunterschriften**,
- den **ersten** und den **letzten Satz** jedes Absatzes,
- **Grafiken**, **Statistiken** und die **Quelle** des Textes.

Scanning: Lesen, um nach bestimmten Informationen zu suchen

Beim **Scanning** suchst du einen Text nach Schlüsselwörtern *(key words)* ab und liest nur dort genauer, wo du sie findest. Das hilft dir, wenn dich nur bestimmte Aspekte eines Themas interessieren. Geh dabei so vor:

Schritt 1: Denk an das Schlüsselwort, nach dem du suchst, oder schreib es auf.

Schritt 2: Geh mit deinen Augen und dem Finger schnell durch den Text, in breiten Schlingen wie bei einem „S" oder „Z" oder von oben nach unten wie bei einem„U". Dabei hast du das Schriftbild oder das Bild der Wörter, nach denen du suchst, vor Augen. Die gesuchten Wörter werden dir sofort „ins Auge springen".

Schritt 3: Wenn das Schlüsselwort, nach dem du suchst, im Text nicht vorkommt, überlege dir, welche anderen Wörter mit den benötigten Informationen zu tun haben, und such nach diesen.

Finding the main ideas of a text

Wie finde ich die Hauptaussagen eines Textes?

1. Jeder Text dreht sich um ein Thema oder hat eine Hauptaussage, z. B. *This summer we've been raising money for the Hickery Soup Kitchen.* Diese Hauptaussage findest du oft im **ersten Absatz**. Lies ihn deshalb besonders gründlich durch.
2. Die Hauptaussage wird in der Regel durch weitere Aussagen bzw. Gedanken unterstützt, z. B. *To raise money we've been to two churches.* Du findest sie oft im ersten oder letzten Satz der nachfolgenden Absätze.
3. Diese weiteren Aussagen bzw. Gedanken werden oft durch Beispiele und Begründungen ergänzt, z. B. *Lots of people have donated ... Altogether we've raised $427.*

SPEAKING AND WRITING SKILLS ▸ *pp. 132–133*

SF REVISION Paraphrasing

Worum geht es beim Paraphrasing?

Paraphrasing bedeutet, etwas mit anderen Worten zu erklären. Das ist hilfreich, wenn dir ein bestimmtes Wort nicht einfällt oder wenn dein Gegenüber dich nicht verstanden hat (siehe auch , S. *76*, Mediation).

Wie gehe ich beim Paraphrasing vor?

- Man kann mit einem Wort umschreiben, das dieselbe Bedeutung hat: 'To wonder' is the same as 'to ask yourself.' Oder man sagt das Gegenteil:. 'Alive' is the opposite of 'dead.'
- Manchmal braucht man mehrere Wörter, z. B. wenn man etwas beschreibt oder erklären will, wie man es verwendet. Dabei benutzt man ein allgemeines Wort (**general word**) und nennt weitere Eigenschaften. A racing car is a very fast car.
- Oder du umschreibst das Wort mit **... is/are like ...** A chef is like a cook, he or she is the main cook in a restaurant.
- Du kannst auch einen Relativsatz (**relative clause**) verwenden: A garage is a place where cars are checked and repaired.

SF REVISION Brainstorming

Drei verschiedene Brainstorming-Techniken

Technik 1: Making a list

Schreib die Ideen so auf, wie sie dir einfallen, und zwar für jede Idee eine neue Zeile. Lies im zweiten Schritt alle deine Ideen durch. Überlege, welche Ideen davon für dein Thema sinnvoll sind und wie du sie zusammenfassen kannst.

Technik 2: Making a mind map
Leg eine Mindmap an.
- Überlege dafür, welche Oberbegriffe zu deinem Thema passen. Verwende unterschiedliche Farben für jeden Oberbegriff.
- Ergänze jede Idee, die zu einem Oberbegriff passt, auf einem Nebenast. Nimm dafür nur wichtige Schlüsselwörter. Du kannst statt Wörtern auch Symbole verwenden und Bilder ergänzen.

Technik 3: The 5 Ws
Schreib die 5 W-Fragen **Who? What? When? Where? Why?** in eine Tabelle.
Die Ideen, die dir zu der jeweiligen Frage kommen, werden darunter geschrieben.

REVISION WRITING COURSE – Zusammenfassung

▸ *pp. 134–135*

The steps of writing

1. Brainstorming – Ideen sammeln.
2. Schreiben. Dabei achte darauf,
   - deine Sätze zu verbinden und auszubauen (*Writing better sentences*),
   - deinen Text gut zu strukturieren (*Using paragraphs*),
   - bei einem Bericht die 5 Ws abzudecken (*Writing a report*),
3. Deinen Text inhaltlich und sprachlich überprüfen (*Correcting your text*).

Writing better sentences

Linking words

Eine Geschichte klingt interessanter, wenn man die Sätze mit **linking words** miteinander verbindet. Dabei gibt es mehrere Möglichkeiten:
- **Time phrases** wie at 7 o'clock, every morning, in the afternoon, a few minutes later, suddenly.
- **Konjunktionen** wie although, because, but, so ... that, that, when, while.
- **Relativpronomen** wie that und who.

Adjektive und Adverbien

- Mit Adjektiven kannst du eine Person, einen Ort, einen Gegenstand oder ein Erlebnis genauer und interessanter beschreiben. Vergleiche: The man looked into the room. ▸ The young man looked into the empty room.
- Mit Adverbien kannst du beschreiben, **wie** jemand etwas macht: The young man looked nervously into the empty room.

Using paragraphs

Structuring a text

Ein längerer Text ist besser zu verstehen, wenn er mehrere Absätze enthält:
- eine Einleitung (**beginning**) – hier schreibst du, worum es geht,
- einen Hauptteil (**middle**) – hier schreibst du mehr über dein Thema,
- einen Schluss (**end**) – hier bringst du den Text zu einem interessanten Ende.

Topic sentences

Am Anfang eines Absatzes sind kurze, einleitende Sätze (**topic sentences**) gut, weil sie den Lesern sofort sagen, worum es geht, z.B.

4. Orte: My trip to ... was fantastic. / ... is famous for ... / ... is a great place.
5. Personen: ... is funny/interesting/clever ...
6. Aktivitäten: ... is good fun. / Lots of people ... every day.

Wie kann ich meine Absätze interessant gestalten?

- Beginne mit einem interessanten Einstiegssatz: You'll never guess what happened to me today! / Did I tell you that ...?
- Fang für jeden neuen Aspekt einen neuen Absatz an.
- Beende deinen Text mit einer Zusammenfassung oder etwas Persönlichem.

Writing a report – structuring information

Worauf kommt es bei einem Bericht an?

- Gib dem Leser **eine schnelle Orientierung**, was passiert ist.
- Beginne mit **wichtigen Informationen** und gib erst dann Detailinformationen.
- Ein Bericht gibt immer Antworten auf die **5 Ws**: Who? What? When? Where? Why? (bzw. How?)
- Verwende das *simple past*.

Correcting your text

Ein Text ist noch nicht „fertig", wenn du ihn zu Ende geschrieben hast. Du solltest ihn immer mehr als einmal durchlesen:
- einmal, um zu sehen, ob er vollständig und gut verständlich ist,
- noch einmal, um ihn auf Fehler zu überprüfen (**Rechtschreibfehler** / **Grammatikfehler**, s.u.).

Spelling mistakes

Lies deinen Text langsam, Wort für Wort. Wenn du unsicher bist, hilft dir ein Wörterbuch. Beachte folgende Regeln:

Tipp
- Manche Wörter haben Buchstaben, die man nicht spricht, aber schreibt, z. B. **autumn**, **climb**.
- Manchmal ändert sich die Schreibweise, wenn ein Wort eine Endung erhält, z. B. **take** → **taking**, **terrible** → **terribly**, **lucky** → **luckily**, **try** → **tries** (**aber stay** → **stays**), **run** → **running**, **drop** → **dropped**.
- Beim Plural tritt manchmal ein **-e** zum **-s**, z. B. **church** → **churches**.

tomato [tə'mɑːtəʊ], *pl* **tomatoes** Tomate II

wife [waɪf], *pl* **wives** [waɪvz] Ehefrau II

drop (**-pp-**) [drɒp] fallen lassen I

forget (**-tt-**) [fə'get] vergessen I

Grammar mistakes

Diese Tipps helfen dir, typische Fehler zu vermeiden:

Tipp
- Im **simple present** wird in der 3. Person Singular **-s** angehängt: **she knows**
- **Unregelmäßige Verben:** Manche Verben bilden die Formen des *simple past* und des Partizip Perfekt *(past participle)* unregelmäßig z.B. **go – went – gone; buy – bought – bought**. Die unregelmäßigen Formen musst du lernen.
- **Verneinung:** Im *simple present* werden Vollverben mit **don't/doesn't** verneint, im *simple past* mit **didn't**.
- **Satzstellung**: Im Englischen gilt immer (auch im Nebensatz):
  a) subject – verb – object (SVO): ... when **I saw my brother.**
  als **ich meinen Bruder sah.**
  b) Orts- vor Zeitangabe: **I bought a nice book in the city yesterday.**

SPEAKING COURSE – Zusammenfassung

► *pp. 138–139*

Starting and continuing a conversation

Ein Gespräch beginnen

Ein Gespräch auf Englisch zu beginnen ist einfacher, als du vielleicht denkst.
Es gibt immer mehrere Möglichkeiten:
- **wenn du etwas erfragen willst** *(z.B. den Weg oder die Uhrzeit)*: Excuse me, do you know ... • Excuse me, can you tell me ...
- **wenn du jemanden begrüßen möchtest oder kennen lernst**: Hi • Hello oder Good morning • Good evening (bei Erwachsenen) ... Oft kann man das Gespräch dann mit einer allgemeinen Bemerkung weiterführen: Great day today! • Fantastic concert, isn't it? • ...
- **wenn du jemanden wieder triffst**: Hi, ..., how are things? • Hi, how is it going? • Hi, ... Good to see/meet you. • Fine weather today, isn't it?

Tipp
- Oft hört man zur Begrüßung auch How are you? oder How do you do? Es wird nicht erwartet, dass man darauf eine Antwort gibt.
- Am besten sagst du einfach Fine, thanks. How about you?

Ein Gespräch führen

Für den weiteren Verlauf des Gesprächs sind diese Wendungen nützlich:
- **sich vorstellen:** By the way, my name's ... • I'm ... • Nice to meet you.
- **sich kennen lernen:** Have you ... before? • Have you ever ...? • What about you?
- **sich verabschieden:** See you tomorrow/next week. • Bye!

Und wenn du etwas nicht verstanden hast, kannst du immer nachfragen:
Sorry, I didn't get that. • Sorry, can you say that again, please?

Having a job interview

Sich vorbereiten

Auf ein Vorstellungsgespräch musst du dich unbedingt vorbereiten. Du solltest Fragen zu den folgenden Bereichen beantworten können:
- deine Eigenschaften (**personal qualities**), Stärken (**strengths**) und Schwächen (**weaknesses**),
- deine Interessen (**interests**) und Arbeitserfahrungen (**work experience**),
- was dich an dem Jobangebot reizt (**why you're interested in the job**).

Überleg dir auch eigene Fragen, zum Beispiel zu deinem Tätigkeitsbereich (**what you have to do**) oder zur Bezahlung (**the pay**).

Im Vorstellungsgespräch

Im Vorstellungsgespräch ist es wichtig, dass du freundlich bist und dich als positiver und interessierter Mensch präsentierst:
- **bei der Begrüßung:** Hello, nice to meet you. / Good morning...
- **warum du dich beworben hast:** Well, I'm really interested in what you do / ...
- **wenn es um deine Joberfahrungen geht:** I really enjoyed working with ...
- **bei der Verabschiedung:** Goodbye and thank you very much.

Tipp
- Hör gut zu, wenn du etwas gefragt wirst.
- Sprich nicht zu viel, aber auch nicht zu wenig.
- Sprich nicht zu schnell.

Having a discussion

Seine Meinung zum Ausdruck bringen und erklären

1. **Expressing an opinion:** In einer Diskussion ist es gut, wenn du möglichst klar und deutlich sagst, was du zu einer bestimmten Frage denkst: I think ... • I feel ... • In my opinion ...
2. **Giving reasons and examples:** Es ist aber noch wichtiger, dass du Beispiele und Argumente nennst, die deine Meinung unterstützen, um deine Gesprächspartner von deinem Standpunkt zu überzeugen (Because ... • First ... / Second ... • For example ... • Let me explain ...).

Auf andere in einer Diskussion reagieren

1. **Asking for clarification:** Manchmal ist es notwendig nachzuhaken, weil man ein Argument nicht verstanden hat: Could you say that again? • Sorry, but I don't understand what you mean.
2. **Agreeing with someone:** Wenn du die Meinung eines anderen unterstützen willst, kannst du das so zum Ausdruck bringen: I agree (with you/...) • That's a good point. • You're right.
3. **Disagreeing with someone:** Oft widerspricht man nicht direkt, sondern leitet seine Reaktion mit Sorry, ... oder I don't think ... ein. Zeig immer Respekt für die Meinung des oder der anderen. I don' t think you can say ... • I see what you mean but ... • No, that's not right. • Sorry, I don't agree with you • Yes, but ...

Giving a presentation

Useful phrases

1. **Einleitung:** Nenne am Beginn deines Vortrags dein Thema und gib einen kurzen Überblick darüber, worum es in deinem Vortrag geht: The topic of my talk today is ... • I'm going to divide this talk into four sections. • First, I'll give you some general facts about ... • Next I'll look at ... • Finally I'll ...
2. **Während der Präsentation:** Mach deutlich, wenn du einen neuen Abschnitt in deinem Vortrag beginnst. Now please have a look at ... • Now I'd like to draw your attention to ... • As you can see in ...
3. **Schluss:** Am Ende deines Vortrags fass die wichtigsten Punkte zusammen. Frag deine Zuhörer, ob sie etwas nachfragen oder kommentieren möchten. To sum up my talk I ... • Please feel free to ask questions or comment on anything I've said.

MEDIATION SKILLS ▸ p. 141

SF REVISION Mediation

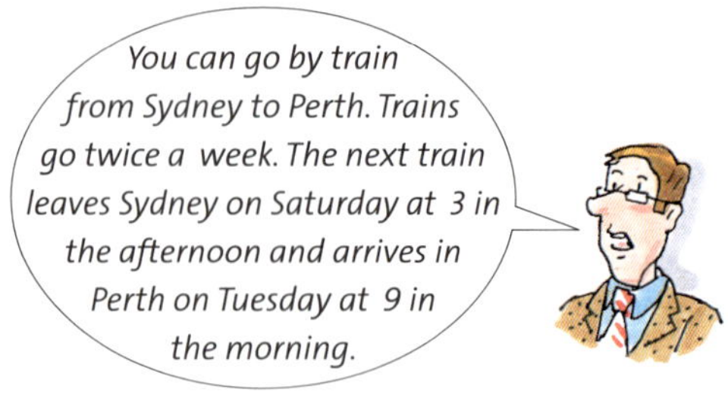

REVISION Worauf muss ich bei mediation achten?

- Übersetze nicht alles wörtlich.
- Gib nur das Wesentliche weiter, lass Unwichtiges weg.
- Verwende kurze und einfache Sätze.
- Wenn du ein Wort nicht kennst, umschreibe es oder ersetze es durch ein anderes Wort.

Was kann ich tun, wenn ich ein wichtiges Wort nicht kenne?

Vielleicht findest du es manchmal schwer, mündliche Aussagen oder schriftliche Textvorlagen in die andere Sprache zu übertragen, z. B. weil

- dein Wortschatz nicht ausreicht,
- dir bekannte Wörter „im Stress" nicht einfallen,
- spezielle Fachbegriffe auftauchen.

Manche Wörter kannst du umschreiben, z. B. mithilfe von Relativsätzen wie:

It's somebody/a person who ... • It's something that you use to ... • It's an animal that ... • It's a place where ...

Schau dir auch den Abschnitt zu Paraphrasing an (S. 72).

Unit 1

GF 4 Indirect speech (I) ▸ p. 149

Indirect speech (reporting verb: simple present) — Zita Wallace says **that** she **saw** terrible things and **that** she **will** never **forget** those first hours.

Indirect speech (reporting verb: simple past) — Zita Wallace said **that** she had seen terrible things. She added **that** she would never forget those first hours.

◂ In der **indirekten Rede** (*indirect* oder *reported speech*) wird berichtet, was jemand sagt oder gesagt hat.
Die indirekte Rede wird mit Verben wie *say, tell sb., add, answer, explain, write* eingeleitet.

◂ Wenn das **einleitende Verb im *simple past*** steht (*she said/told us/explained/answered* usw.), dann werden die Zeitformen der direkten Rede meist verändert: Sie werden um eine Zeitstufe in die Vergangenheit „zurückverschoben" *(backshift of tenses)*.

Veränderungen der Zeitformen bei einleitendem Verb im *simple past*

	Direct speech	Indirect speech
present ▸ past	'I don't care about money.' 'Australia is saying sorry.'	Zita **said** she didn't care about money. The report **said** Australia was saying sorry.
past ▸ past perfect	'I saw terrible things.'	Zita **told** us she had seen terrible things.
can* ▸ *could	'You can go shopping with us.'	The nuns **said** that the girls could go shopping with them.
***will*-future ▸ *would* + infinitive**	'I'll never forget those days.'	Zita **said** she would never forget those days.
***going to*-future ▸ *was/were going to* + infinitive**	'The government is going to apologize.'	They **said** the government was going to apologize.
present perfect ▸ past perfect	'I haven't forgotten that evening.'	Zita **added** that she hadn't forgotten that evening.

Verben im *past perfect* bleiben unverändert, da man sie nicht weiter „zurückverschieben" kann.

Unit 2

GF 5 Indirect speech (II)

► p. 150

5.1 Commands and requests

Simon Look for clothes for the interview. And don't be shy.
Simon told them to look for clothes for the interview. And he told them not to be shy.
Simon Mani, please choose a new tie.
Simon asked Mani to choose a new tie.

◄ **Aufforderungen, Anordnungen** und **Ratschläge** werden in der indirekten Rede meist mit ***tell sb. to do sth.*** (bzw. ***tell sb. not to do sth.***) wiedergegeben.

◄ Eine **Bitte** wird meist mit ***ask sb. to do sth.*** (bzw. ***ask sb. not to do sth.***) wiedergegeben.

5.2 Questions

Direct question (with question word)	What do you know about my business?
Indirect question	Rita asked Mani **what** he knew about her business.
Direct question (yes/no question)	Do you have any weaknesses?
Indirect question	Rita asked him **if** he had any weaknesses.

◄ Wenn die direkte **Frage mit einem Fragewort** beginnt (*what, when, where, why, how* usw.), dann wird das Fragewort in der indirekten Frage beibehalten.

◄ Handelt es sich bei der direkten Frage um eine **Frage ohne Fragewort** *(yes/no question)*, dann wird die indirekte Frage mit ***if*** („ob") eingeleitet.

Unit 3

GF 6 Participles

► p. 151

6.1 REVISION Participle forms

Present participle *(-ing)*:

play	→ **playing**	try	→ **trying**
phone	→ **phoning**	plan	→ **planning**

Past participle, regular verbs *(-ed)*:

play	→ **played**	try	→ **tried**
phone	→ **phoned**	plan	→ **planned**

Past participle, irregular verbs:

go	→ **gone**	make	→ **made**
take	→ **taken**	write	→ **written**

◄ Das **Partizip Präsens** *(present participle)* bildet man durch Anhängen von ***-ing*** an den Infinitiv. Beachte die Besonderheiten bei der Schreibung.

◄ Das **Partizip Perfekt** *(past participle)* eines regelmäßigen Verbs wird durch Anhängen von ***-ed*** an den Infinitiv gebildet. Beachte auch hier die Besonderheiten bei der Schreibung.

Bedenke, dass unregelmäßige Verben eigene 3. Formen haben, die man einzeln lernen muss.

Additional information

6.2 Participle clauses instead of relative clauses

1 Shane saw posters **showing his picture.**
... Poster, die sein Bild zeigten.
2 Now Shane is a reliable young man **looking for work.** ... zuverlässiger junger Mann, der Arbeit sucht.
3 The photos **sent to people in his area** showed a 14-year-old trouble-maker.
... die Fotos, die den Leuten in seiner Gegend geschickt wurden, ...

Partizipialsätze können Relativsätze ersetzen.

◄ Partizipialsätze mit ***present participle*** (Sätze **1** und **2**) entsprechen Relativsätzen im **Aktiv**:

1 ... ***showing*** *his picture* = ... ***which showed*** *his picture*
2 ... ***looking*** *for work* = ... ***who is looking*** *for work*

◄ Partizipialsätze mit ***past participle*** (Satz **3**) entsprechen Relativsätzen im **Passiv**:

3 ... ***sent*** *to people in his area* = ... ***that were sent*** *to people* ...

GF 7 The passive

7.2 Form

Das Passiv bildet man mit einer **Form von *be*** und der 3. Form des Verbs (Partizip Perfekt, *past participle*).

The passive

Simple present: ***am/are/is*** + past participle	So much trash is thrown into the springs. So viel Müll wird in die Quellen geworfen.
Simple past: ***was/were*** + past participle	I was beaten by my best friend. Ich wurde von meinem besten Freund besiegt.
Present perfect: ***have/has been*** + past participle	A lot of coins and bills have been donated. Eine Menge Münzen und Noten sind gespendet worden.
will*-future:** ***will be + past participle	The food will be given to the Soup Kitchen tomorrow. Morgen werden die Lebensmittel der Suppenküche übergeben (werden).
Modal auxiliaries: ***can/must/should/... be*** + past participle	The food can be stored there overnight. Die Lebensmittel können dort über Nacht gelagert werden. Something must be done / should be done to help people in need. Es muss / sollte etwas getan werden, ...

Unit 4

GF 8 Conditional sentences ▸ *p. 153*

8.1 REVISION Type 1 and type 2

If you run, you'll catch the bus.
Wenn du rennst, kriegst du den Bus noch.

If you miss the bus, you can take / should take / must take a taxi.
Wenn du den Bus verpasst, kannst/sollst/musst du ein Taxi nehmen.

if-Satz (Bedingung)	Hauptsatz (Folge)
If you run,	*you'll catch the bus.*
If you miss the bus,	*you can take a taxi.*
simple present	**– *will-future* – *can/should/must* + Infinitiv**

If you ran, you would catch the bus.
Wenn du rennen würdest, würdest du den Bus noch kriegen.
If you caught the bus, you could be home in time for dinner.
Wenn du den Bus kriegen würdest, könntest du rechtzeitig zum Abendessen daheim sein.

if-Satz (Bedingung)	Hauptsatz (Folge)
If you ran,	*you would catch/could catch/ might catch the bus.*
simple past	***would/could/might* + Infinitiv**

Additional information

8.2 Type 3

If you had run, you would have caught the bus.
Wenn du gerannt wärst, hättest du den Bus noch gekriegt.
If you had caught the bus, you could have had dinner with us.
Wenn du den Bus gekriegt hättest, hättest du mit uns Abendbrot essen können.

if-Satz (Bedingung)	Hauptsatz (Folge)
If you had run,	*you would have caught/ could have caught the bus.*
past perfect	***would/could* + *have* + Partizip Perfekt**

1 LISTENING Summer vacation
1 B; *2* B; *3* C; *4* C; *5* B; *6* B

2 LISTENING A day in the life of …
a) Why bushfires start
b) *1* F; *2* T; *3* F; *4* T; *5* F; *6* T; *7* T; *8* F; *9* T; *10* F; *11* T

3 READING Sydney for everyone
a) Sydney's sights
b) Opening times, Sights
c) *1* T; *2* F; *3* N; *4* T; *5* F; *6* N; *7* T; *8* F; *9* F; *10* N; *11* F; *12* T; *13* T; *14* N

4a) WRITING An e-mail
Hi/Dear …
Here I am in fantastic Sydney!
Yesterday was a sightseeing day, so it was really interesting. First we went to see the famous Harbour Bridge. People were climbing it, but that isn't for me. After that we went to The Rocks, which is an old area with colonial buildings, souvenir shops and cafés too. After that we saw the Opera House – really amazing – but we didn't have time for a tour. In the afternoon we did a harbour trip and we sailed under the Bridge. That was better than climbing it! Tomorrow will be a Bondi Beach day, so we'll have to 'slip, slop, slap' because it's pretty hot here.
I'll write again tomorrow evening and tell you more news! …

4b) WRITING A summary
The story is about Nina, her brother David and two friends who drive to Kakadu National Park to celebrate Nina's birthday. While they are driving, they argue about the danger of saltwater crocodiles for tourists. David thinks they should be really careful because park rangers cannot guarantee visitor safety, but Nina says David is too scared. That evening they celebrate Nina's birthday and next morning they leave for Jim Jim Falls. Nina and Mike want to go swimming there. When they are climbing over the rocks, David hurts his foot and can't continue. He is worried because they lose Nina and Mike, so Cathy tries to calm him. When the two return, Nina is very quiet. Later she tells David about a huge saltie at the falls and how scared she was. She apologizes to David because she knows he was right and she was stupid. She asks him not to tell their parents.

5a) SPEAKING Travelling
1 Hi/Hello. What can you see on the Uluru tours, please?
2 What time do you have to get up, and when does the tour start?
3 How long does the tour take?
4 Do we get breakfast on the tour?
5 How much does the tour cost and what do you get for the price?
6 I'd like to book the tour for tomorrow, for two adults and two teenagers, please.

5b) SPEAKING Travelling
Picture A:
Picture A shows a scene in the outback with two people, a white camping bus on the right and a small white tent in the foreground on the left. The man is sitting on the front of the camping bus looking at the sky, and the woman is sitting on a camping chair. The sky is bright red, so maybe the sun is going down. There's nothing in the background, only red earth for miles. There's nothing green, no plants or bushes. The people look very relaxed. Maybe they're tired after a hot day of driving. It seems to be very lonely and quiet, maybe even boring. They're wearing shorts, so it's probably still hot. They've put up the tent before it gets dark. Maybe they're thinking how beautiful, but how dangerous the outback can be.

6 MEDIATION Berlin tours
Alpha tours – Berlin: tours by bus, bike or on foot, every day; groups – all sizes; modern buses and new bikes; highlights – Brandenburg Gate, Checkpoint Charlie, small part of the Berlin Wall, TV tower, Berlin Cathedral, Charlottenburg Palace and more; tours morning, afternoon and evening, breaks and meal on day tours, guides speak foreign languages, see website for details

Skills Check 2 Lösungen/Musterlösungen

1 LISTENING First day at work
1 B; *2* A; *3* B; *4* A; *5* B; *6* B; *7* C; *8* A

2 READING Jobs
a) Young people describing jobs that they do.
b) *1* D; *2* A; *3* B; *4* F; *5* E
c) *1* Nick *2* Sam *3* Lauren *4* Lucy *5* Nick *6* Adam *7* Sam *8* Sam

3 WRITING A formal letter
...
Dear Sir/Madam
I read your advertisement in the ... of ... about summer jobs for German-speaking students with the London Tourist Service. I would like to apply and am enclosing my CV in English.
As you can see from my CV, I already have some work experience in Germany. I have a good level of spoken English and I enjoy meeting people and helping customers. I am friendly, reliable and a good team worker.
Could you please answer the following questions? Would your company help with somewhere to stay? What would the working hours be? Could you please tell me how much I would earn? I would be available for work for 6 weeks from 1st July.
I look forward to hearing from you.
Yours faithfully ...

4 WRITING Your CV
Individual answers. Check with the CVs on pp. 38–39 of your student's book.

5 WRITING An informal letter
Hi ...!
I must tell you about an ad that I read today. The London Tourist Service needs German students for summer jobs – and I have applied!
I think working away from home would be good for me – and for my English. But first I want to know more about the jobs, working hours, free time, where I would stay, and so on.
I'd really like to work in London. It would look good on my CV. I might make some new friends and maybe I could visit you in my free time. But maybe the work will be hard, with long hours, bad pay and not much free time ...
I'll let you know if they answer. I'm quite excited!
Love ...

6a) SPEAKING Jobs and work experience
Picture 1 shows a tourist guide on a London sightseeing bus. He is probably telling tourists about the history of the city and its buildings. Maybe the tourists aren't listening to everything he says. I think it's quite a good job because you are outside a lot and you meet a lot of people. But it's the same work every day, like most jobs. The guide probably says exactly the same things to all his tourist groups, and he does the same tour at the same time every day. He probably feels bored, but he always has to be friendly.

Picture 2 shows office workers at their computers in a large office. They are probably not very happy. It think it's hard to think and work when there are so many people in one room. There's always background noise when people are phoning, chatting, walking around, when telephones are ringing, etc. The workers are never private. Everybody sees and hears what they do – the boss too.
I would like to do the job of the tourist guide because I think it's more relaxing. Riding round London in a bus is better than sitting at a computer all day.

6b) SPEAKING Jobs and work experience
I think work experience is important because you learn a lot about the world of work. You have to be punctual, reliable, confident and hard-working. You meet different kinds of people. You learn skills that are important for your job later, like organisation, telephone skills, team work, maybe new computer skills.
I have some work experience in a book shop and at a petrol station. I liked serving customers and chatting to them. But it was boring at the petrol station between customers. I like to be with people.
I don't have a job at the moment because I have to work hard for school now.
My favourite school subjects are German, English and Maths. I like reading and I am interested in languages. My grades are good too. When I leave school, I'd like to work in a bank or in a hotel.

7 MEDIATION Small ads
1 Job in a café: you can work 3 hours morning or afternoon, have to work in kitchen and café preparing vegetables, doing tables, serving ice cream in garden, good pay
2 Job in hotel (near cathedral): you can work part-time or hourly, have to answer phone calls in English and look after foreign guests, needn't have experience of hotel work, above average pay
3 Job with American family: have to look after children, afternoons, don't have to do housework, needn't have a driving licence
4 Job giving English conversation classes to small groups: 2 hours twice a week mornings, don't have to speak German